Testimonials

David's book is an easy read for those who want digital transformation to help our business. In his book, he clearly sets out guidelines and proven insights taken from his experience. His over-riding message is that the heart of any positive transformation is people. I would recommend this book to anyone in business, no matter what the business.

Lesley Gillespie, co-founder of Bakers Delight

As businesses struggle with how best to embrace the opportunities provided by new digital technologies, this timely reference text provides practical and important guidance that everyone should read. David's combination of strategic thinking and practical experience provides the reader with unique insights.

Ian Hancock, partner-in-charge of KPMG's
Management Consulting Group Australia

Intelligent Automation (the rise of the digital worker) will transform our workplace: every activity, every role, every job automated or augmented by AI. In Industry 4.0, we are in a permanent state of transformation. Why, then, are executives not giving attention to those hard-learned lessons of successful change that David discusses in this timely and readable book? Industry 4.0 is about people and robots. That's a change that is hard, so we need to reflect and think about it—as David does here.

Mike Hobday, former general manager of Automation Europe, IBM

I've known David for many years and have worked with him on the international circuit. His unique professional journey has given him a broad perspective. This book is a collection of his reflections and how technology can be used to unlock value. In a busy world, this is worth a read.

Tim Hynes, CIO of Allied Irish Banks

David presents a compelling argument that digital is, and should be, everyone's business to ensure that intelligent technologies deliver on their promise. He highlights the need for thoughtful change based on his tapestry of experience in technology and business. A really easy and practical read with concepts accessible to all, and written with honesty and humour.

Dr Lisa Interligi, chief human resources & corporate services officer at CIMIC Group Limited

David's deep experience as a technology leader shines through in the relevant and practical advice in this book. Importantly, driving or responding to digital disruption is ultimately all about the people in the organisation. This is highlighted throughout: humble leaders who treat others with respect and build aligned teams with shared values. I'd love to work in such an organisation.

Leigh Jasper, co-founder and CEO at Aconex

Though more and more business executives are talking about digital or digitalisation of their business, I have observed that not many of them can clearly articulate a meaningful strategy. This book has provided us a unique model (D-I-R-T-Y). It is thoughtful and pragmatic. We can use it to be more sustainable and to avoid the traps of 'transformation' in a meaningful digital future. "Digital will be part of business but not all of the business" and "Transitions are better than Transformations" are wisdoms drawn from David's rich experiences and insights in delivery of real Relevance between digital and overall business. These offer guidance to all executives, particularly CIOs. I continue to believe that people will become more important in the digital future, and we need to empower and enable them more. Let us try to be Lighthouse leaders. Let us try to make changes, every day, to create a better life.

Dr LU Jianzhong, chairman of John Holland Board and chairman of CCCI

Having read David's book, there is no argument that technology has and will continue to change how organisations operate. There is also no argument that the 'human element' is crucial to an organisation's success. David draws on his deep practical experience to highlight how organisations can't ignore the promise and potential of new digital strategies, but at the same time, it would be negligent to dismiss the value of great talent and high-functioning teams.

Mark Korda, co-founder and partner of KordaMentha

David's book has been triggered by the digital transformation but it delves more into human actions and interactions. The author draws on his extensive experience to put forth a model that will ferment successful businesses in a digitalised world. He does so candidly and with humour.

Dr Theodore Modis, author of Predictions: Conquering Uncertainty

This must-read book highlights the importance of simplicity and transparency within an organisation in bridging the organisation's strategies and goals with digital initiatives. This is the key to making things happen and getting results.

Rob Monaci, CEO of Georgiou

This book provides real insight for those who want to achieve successful change in a technology-dependent world. In this excellent book, David reminds us that in our complex and ever-changing corporate lives, our future is still dependent on people and relationships, and not just clever technology. David is a leader in the true sense; he is able to achieve great outcomes through people engagement and future vision.

Paul Newham, executive general manager of service delivery at CBA, former COO of Westpac

Disruption, change and transformation comes naturally to some, while others struggle. Those who struggle, will die (well, not literally). This book unpacks key success criteria in a way that is refreshing and clear. David has always been an expansive thinker and a collaborator at heart, and this book is a prime example of the fruits of his approach.

Rob Phillpot, co-founder of Aconex

Digital transformation projects are hard. As David points out: many will fail. This book is the essential tactical companion to decode the digital journey. David draws on his long personal experience at the cutting edge of going digital to deliver a thought-provoking and jargon-free view on the psychology and processes best deployed to maximise the chances of success.

Gavin Smith, head of technology, media and
telecommunications and partner at Allens

Wrestling with this topic is going to be essential for all leaders who want to make their businesses relevant in the future. Recognising that it is about mindset, approach, customers, colleagues, and technology will allow leaders to deal with all interconnected aspects and have a chance of winning. David forces us to wrestle with our own personal perspectives and challenges us to recognise that we need to go on a mission to learn and adjust. Everything written here has been lived first-hand by David; he has made his mistakes and he has had his wins, and the results of those learnings are presented here for us to start from a higher level of understanding ... if we choose to.

David Whiteing, Group COO of Standard Chartered Bank

DIGITAL IS EVERYONE'S BUSINESS

DIGITAL
IS EVERYONE'S
BUSINESS

A guide to transition

DAVID BANGER

davidbanger

Copyright © David Banger 2019

All models copyright © David Banger 2019

First published in 2019 in Melbourne

Edited by Joanna Yardley at The Editing House

Typeset and cover design by BookPOD

Printed and bound in Australia by BookPOD

ISBN: 978-0-6486968-0-3 (pbk) 978-0-6486968-1-0 (e-book)

A catalogue record for this book is available from the National Library of Australia

*This book is dedicated to **every** former colleague, thank you.*

CONTENTS

ABOUT DAVID

There are many reasons why I don't like writing in the third person, but this little piece reads much better if I do.

David believes that within organisations, *good* people have the potential to be *great* and that their current knowledge—combined with digital fundamentals—will contribute to a business's potential.

David is an author, adjunct professor, former CIO and digital executive. David lived in London from 2001 to 2010 and is now based in Melbourne, Australia. He was employed across many industries including Construction and Engineering, Professional Services, Technology, Management Consulting and Financial Services being both Banking and Insurance. Much of David's career involved transformation and the next stage of something. An internationally recognised innovator, he is a thinker and pragmatist.

His expertise lies in offering unique and succinct insights that enable organisations and their people to realise their technology and digital potential. He now works with CEOs, Executives, CIOs and their teams who are committed to realising the potential of their technology. He founded CHANGE lead | Practical Digital in 2018 to do this.

David's career began unorthodoxly. He left high school at sixteen without completing his high school certificate. He returned to formal education in his twenties, where he gained under- and post-graduate (MBA) qualifications. Since 2015, he has been a member of the Business School Industry Advisory Board and an Adjunct Professor at Swinburne University of Technology.

Computerworld named David as a global Premier Technology Leader in 2016.

In 2018, he completed IMD and MIT's Driving Strategic Innovation in Switzerland and he is an advocate of their approach to practise-based research and refers to this with his clients.

Digital nuances

Things that mattered less in the past matter more now. Since 1660, my family's surname has been Banger, pronounced Bain-ger. This was not our family's original surname. A relative completed a family tree and discovered my distant relatives left France at the time Charles II returned to the United Kingdom upon the restoration of the monarchy. The research uncovered that our family surname was originally Bonjour. This was anglicised to Banger when they arrived in the United Kingdom.

For previous generations, the incorrect pronunciation by people was completely understandable. Although when they were prompted to think 'danger', 'stranger' or 'ranger' when pronouncing Banger ... aha! ... the intended pronunciation stuck.

Back then, people met more physically. That provided the opportunity for my ancestors to introduce themselves in person and offer the appropriate pronunciation. In an electronic world, the instances of this are considerably less frequent as we all meet electronically prior to meeting physically.

I don't mind the incorrect pronunciation. In fact, it makes me more memorable. Sometimes I don't bother correcting it if it is a one-off interaction. However, my children now live in this electronic world. The 'i' added to their surname is a small nuance that will save them the endless explanations.

Consider this story a metaphor for this book. When reading it, think about the nuances, the details, the little things that if left as they are or undertaken over time, will either subtract from or contribute to much bigger things.

A NOTE FROM DAVID

I should declare that I enjoy thinking and writing about technology in business. Some of the ideas in this book have stayed with me until now. Some have been shared in a weekly blog I wrote for many years as a C-level executive. The blogs endeavoured to simplify the complex. The interactions, after posting my blog, were valuable beyond the connection with a colleague; they helped evolve and refine my thinking. The blogs were written for a business audience, not the technology teams I managed, although they assisted the teams in understanding my thinking and our priorities. This book is intended for both a business and technology audience. The approach is not binding (you will not die if it's not followed). It utilises concepts that can be applied within the proposed structure or independently. I have tested and used many of these concepts on several occasions. Seek to use what you see fit—if something works, please let me know. I like practise-based research and am always open to learning.

Throughout this book, I have referenced other authors, journals, articles and events that have inspired me. Each external reference provides validation, inspiration and relevance to the point I am making. I like different experiences and to consume content; it improves my thinking. In the past, I have written about consumption junkies, those who consume everything and do nothing. This book is a balance between sharing experiences, information, a framework and optional actions.

> 'The first Apple was just a
> culmination of my whole life.'
> —Steve Wozniak

This book, in many ways, is a story of my professional life; it's filled with things I have experienced and learned that have shaped me. At one of my former employers, the CEO asked for all communication to be written as if it were being printed on the front page of *The Sun* newspaper in London and for there to be facts but also include a story. We all were asked to write our professional stories. The book also makes no reference to specific technology; this is a deliberate decision. A former vice president who led our much-loved international department once said, 'The technology will come and then go but the people and this business will remain. That is where the excellence starts'. Both have stayed with me (plus many other things).

Additionally, I seek to use words as memorable banners or strap lines. This is not marketing; at some stage, it may be used within my marketing content; however, this is not their purpose. These words, when combined with stories of my professional experiences, are memorable and prompt action or recollection when the reader encounters a certain situation. Some of my former colleagues will notice these, some have evolved from when they were first introduced, and I expect they will continue to do so.

My career has had two halves: PT and IT. IT is not short for information technology (that's just a quirky coincidence); rather it's short for *in-tech*. And PT is not for part time; it's *pre-tech*. I am a business person who discovered his passion for the potential of technology halfway through his career. I am fortunate enough to have been employed by seven companies (one of these twice), to have lived abroad for nine years and to have worked in many countries. My career decisions were made on the foundation of learning rather than remaining where I was. At times, this may have confused some former colleagues; however, these experiences have manifested in this book and where I am professionally today.

We live in a world of extremes; this is possibly due to the volume of data being produced. Things are sensationalised to capture our attention. Everything appears to be a sprint or a crisis and this dilutes the things that truly are significant. This book will not sensationalise or create a burning platform. It is intended to put into perspective and moderate the potential of digital. There are those who think everything will be disrupted; some of these people offer 'hope' through their professional services that they will find 'the answer' and subsequent actions for your organisation. I don't subscribe to this; this book is intended to improve thinking and contemplation of options prior to your team acting. I believe in thinking more to do less and maximising the opportunity of being and doing the best we can in any situation.

Further, I believe there remains an opportunity for organisations to 'think global' and 'act local'.

There is a general industry belief that your organisation should be the disruptor prior to being disrupted. I also don't believe that. However, your organisation will not remain in the form it is in today. There is no doubt that it will need to shift and transition but possibly not transform. Many transformation initiatives fail. Many studies indicate there is only a 10 to 20% probability of success. Why would you choose to do something that is unlikely to work?

There is a lot of information on digital, and I have consumed more than my fair portion of it. I have been at the digital buffet. Although there are learnings that can be applied, digital will *be part of* business, not *all of the* business. There is a dedicated digital section within this book; however, there are steps to get to digital. In some ways, I believe that your digital potential will not be realised unless you are ready. Like many things, you should prepare prior to undertaking them.

This book offers a series of building blocks or phases. You will need to consider if this 'preparation' is required to optimise your digital undertaking. These phases integrate my experiences and include knowledge from others offering insight for contemplation and options to commence a shift—a transition. Transitions are better than transformations. If you are reading this book, it is likely that transitions may be underway, some are in 'thought' stage and there is a desire to identify others.

This book is about more than digital; it is about your team being ready and fit for your future.

Digital is everyone's business.

INTRODUCTION

Imagine having 20:20 digital hindsight for the 2020s

The 2020s loom large for organisations and many are considering their digital strategies. Many have digital intentions but are uncertain of what needs to be actioned. There are a range of opportunities for organisations willing to explore their digital potential and consequences for organisations continuing a traditional path.

Are you getting your hands dirty? This can have two meanings:

1. You have become involved in something where the realities might compromise your principles.

2. You are stuck in an ivory tower dictating strategy but are prepared to put in the effort and hard work to make the details actually happen.

The book aims to help avoid the first and enable the second. I use the D-I-R-T-Y acronym to outline the sections of this book. Each section is part of a sequence that will enable digital and subsequent transitions in an organisation.

- **D**igital: Timing, thinking differently, what needs to be considered to help achieve greater clarity? When is the right time for your product to enter the market? What is your digital business model? How are you differentiating in a digital world? Why does your perspective of business need to evolve?

- **I**nnovation: What lessons can you learn from the past? How can you make them part of your future? What could be tactically implemented immediately? How can the efforts of longer-term aspirations be broken into parts?

- **R**elevance: This covers a range of topics, from rightsizing the organisation, managing careers, practice and culture of risk, and how all this can help reduce the probability of a catastrophe and avoid situations 'where the realities might compromise your principles'. Plus, it explores why you should maintain a level of relevance with the broader market as an organisation and an individual.

- **T**echnology: What needs to be in place for credibility and confidence? How transparency can create understanding and circumstances for meaningful business contribution.

- **Y**our mindset: How your past experiences prejudice your future. What is your mindset? How work is approached in your organisation and why this now needs to be different. Thinking is now more important than doing.

When applying the above framework, we work backwards. We start with you and your organisation's mindset—without the right mindset, it will be difficult to step through the other sections.

A meaningful digital future

Let's fast forward ...

It's 2020-something and your organisation has continued to be just in time for your market. It's not out on a limb waiting for the market to catch up nor is it working a hunch—it's at the sweet spot. This has been achieved through the integration of your existing traditional business and the timely emergence of digital products and services. *Things were different a few years ago. The team was always scrambling to understand what was going on. Upon determining what was happening, your organisation either ignored it, or played the catch-up game with a token effort that had suboptimal offerings compared to others.*

In the 2020s, the people within your organisation are connected yet diverse. They all *think* but are not all thinking the same, and ideas are welcomed and refined by the group. There is no hierarchy; those people who can offer the greatest contribution to something are empowered and supported. There is a spirit of learning; people are exploring rather than knowing. The search of knowledge within the organisation is one of the foundation stones, but there are other stones too. The backlog of work has been rationalised. People are celebrated for their quality of thought rather than their volume of work. There is a willingness from people to place the organisation and colleagues first rather than calculate how to survive or shine.

The technology team has been a key contributor to the digital outcomes; it is transparent, forthright and can be counted on to deliver its piece of these emerging digital services. *This was not always the case. The technology team was a bit of a black box and engaged only when dragged to the table. There was inconsistency of services and the employee experience was poor and sometimes drove a lack of trust.* The technology team now openly communicates regularly, explaining initiatives and how the team is linked to the bigger picture. The team offers timely thinking that is relevant and helps progress outcomes sooner. The business wouldn't want it any other way.

The organisation is more relevant at many levels. This relevance has been achieved through sensible risk management practices; the people within the organisation know how to manage a risk and escalate when required. Your people are capable risk professionals and are no longer dependent on resources outside their team. The risk escalations from a team result in people swarming to help and not judge a situation. *Those dark days of judgement and competitive behaviour, of ensuring the other team was not doing as well as yours, no longer exist.*

Teams are proactively suggesting how they should evolve rather than waiting for those former reorganisations that were never quite right, always requiring a revisit a year later. People can focus on their work and career and not on how they can keep their job. Some of your people have a genuine presence in the market; they are sought out to share their experiences at events and in other industries. There is a true sense of pride in being part of this organisation. When your people are approached for roles at other organisations, they decline them. Their current role and how it's undertaken makes this organisation unique. In many ways, things have just started, and people want to be part of the future.

There are parallels in how the organisation operates with great companies of the past. Everyone is aware of and respects our organisation's past; however, we have changed the future trajectory by learning from these great companies. There is a shared understanding that ideas are not out of the blue, they are a result of a group of people committed to not settling for the status quo. Ideas are evolved by groups of people and shared with the relevant external audiences. They are refined prior to release, they are not perfected, but they are appropriate, practical and better than many. There have been occasions when the team has operated with restricted circumstances, 'we have been up against it'. These situations galvanised the group; the shared experience has brought people together, *unlike in the past when things were terse, tense and people blamed one another.*

Your teams know their core capabilities and possible limitations; they are smart and partner with other external organisations with the capabilities needed. Your teams are not led into these arrangements by others, they are aware of the capabilities and initiate the specific interaction. The external partner's capability complements the organisation's capability, creating scale and reducing time to outcomes. There are partners who have been present within your organisation for a considerable period. *This is not like the arrangements of the past, when a partner was brought in to save something and it often ended badly.*

Finally, your organisation is constantly shifting not sprinting. *In the past, there was a sprint and then rest routine as transformation efforts were massive and almost always missed the objectives.* Today, the organisation is constantly shifting; it is always in transition. You are closer to your customer and the activities behind the scenes are more integrated. You are realising your potential.

How was this achieved?

PART 1

YOUR MINDSET

Organisations continue with non-value adding work

Potential outcomes are eroded by work that is no longer relevant (or soon to be irrelevant).

Employees have been conditioned to *attract* and *attach* themselves to work. Scandals within industries have created more work. Businesses have 'physical spaces' like stores and 'digital places' like apps and a website. Often, employees interact with these 'digital experiences' in a traditional and manual manner to get the work done. These are just some of the circumstances that have added to the work of an employee, but are often seen as not very valuable.

There is an imbalance of thinking within organisations where the focus is on common initiatives across the organisation rather than the specifics of the work within the organisation. People will participate with these common initiatives. They are like a day out; however, they soon return home to their work. The potential of these initiatives often isn't realised as they only skim the surface and don't get to the root of the issue and how people think about their work.

Your Mindset is the foundation cornerstone. It either enables or confirms the following elements have been considered or are in place:

- Elimination of non-value adding work.
- Thinking about the work prior to committing to it.
- The importance of second order change, evolving to sustainable situations.
- The benefits of rationalising responsibilities, activities and initiatives.

- Ignorance awareness and the pitfalls of being digitally dumb or numb.

- The alignment of teams, creating an environment of deep engagement.

**

This section of the book details an approach that profiles work within organisations and links this to their digital potential. The approach establishes if the mindset to work within an organisation is:

- Undertaking: Individual and reactive traditional work.

- Lounging: A collective community that is comfortable with the work as it is.

- Sole exploring: Individuals choosing to explore options for work in isolation.

- Making meaning: An organisation with a greater purpose and contemporary work.

The importance of employees in determining the nature of their work and any remediation is the key to shifting the organisation. Their involvement will change and then sustain the organisation, enabling a constant state of transitions and potentially averting significant transformations.

Finally, organisations are at risk of not realising their digital potential while traditional, irrelevant or soon-to-be irrelevant work continues. Further, organisations are often fragmented with emerging work being developed in isolation.

Growth mindset

> 'Always remember—your focus
> determines your reality.'
>
> —George Lucas

Let's begin with the end in mind.

In their book, *What's Your Digital Business Model?*, MIT researchers Weill and Woerner (2018) delve into digital businesses and industries. They indicate that the future is here but it is not yet evenly distributed. Below are some facts they have scattered throughout their book.

- Enterprises in the top third of digital customer experience had 8.5% higher net profit margins and 7.8% higher revenue growth than their competitors.

- Industry analyses of content, customer experience and platforms found that the top third of financial performers in the financial services industry had 29%, 35% and 26% better content, customer experience and platform scores respectively. The IT and services industry had the highest industry scores; whereas, energy, mining and healthcare scored poorly. The industries that scored poorly have an opportunity, while organisations within industries that scored strongly will need to consider differentiation (more on this in Part 5).

- Many board members perceived digital disruption as one of their biggest threats, estimating that 32% of revenues will be threatened in the next five years; interestingly, only 39% of board members specifically discussed the digitisation of their enterprises' business models.

There are different mindsets towards going digital within industries and different paces in organisations within industries. This indicates there will be a diverse range of views in various departments within organisations.

There is not one single initiative that cuts through digital; instead, there are likely to be many initiatives that edge closer to a digital outcome, and there will be lessons to be learned throughout such efforts. Learning is paramount, and a growth mindset enables learning. The efforts will be incremental, various and will contribute to an outcome.

> 'The illiterate of the 21st century will not be those who cannot read and write, but those who cannot learn, unlearn, and relearn.'
> —Alvin Toffler

In Carol Dweck's study (outlined in her 2007 book *Mindset*: *The New Psychology of Success*), students responded differently to failure in that some rebounded while others were devastated. When a student believed they could become smarter, they understood that effort would lead to greater achievements. People's mindsets can shift from fixed to growth. When this occurs, it leads to increased motivation and achievement. Leaders within organisations will need to learn from their organisation and their external contexts to realise their businesses' digital potential.

Decisions made on a gut feeling or experience now need to be replaced with the skills of questioning, reflecting and facilitating. The decisions will be supported with data. As a result, organisational relationships will be closer, analysis will be more prevalent, and details will become clearer. In visiting

Facebook, one of many memorable insights was its mantra 'data wins arguments'.

Data, when combined with collective thought, is a building block for innovation (more on this later) and when combined with an external context, organisations can be more decisive. Collective thought is not consensus, conversations need to be facilitated to collect the thinking. Note this is collecting and not calibrating thinking. Leaders, within organisations that operate in this manner, should seek to initially increase the overall quality of thought among their immediate colleagues and their direct reports within an organisation. When undertaken consistently over time, this behaviour will be replicated by others (becoming a cultural norm), creating a capable group of people that will constantly shift the organisation and potentially averting the need for significant transformation.

In an organisation, a collective growth mindset with a thirst for data is the first step to shifting an organisation's digital capability and its people's digital contribution.

Current work is *not* the future

The intersect of the 'physical space' and the 'digital place' present an opportunity for organisations to evolve. This opportunity will be missed if organisations continue to think in the same manner.

There are many articles that consider things such as the linking of the physical property, human resources and technology strategies: why open-plan offices are not the answer and how many future roles will be automated etc. The articles and research is interesting and valuable; however, I have always been frustrated by a piece that was almost always missing—the work within an organisation. There are considerably fewer articles on the work undertaken within organisations and why this work is being completed. This is possibly due to the complexity within organisations and the challenge of getting a grasp of what is happening.

Organisations invest a considerable amount of time, energy and money on physical places and digital spaces; however, there is an insufficient effort on how organisations could be helping their people think differently about their work. Beyond evolving a place or space within an organisation, there is an opportunity to consider how people can be enabled to 'think' about their work rather than just 'complete' their work.

Firstly, let's consider what has happened, this century, to condition current employee thinking:

- Organisations have continued to shed roles, and the responsibilities of those roles have been consolidated into fewer roles; therefore, people are juggling the work and attaching themselves to it so they can remain employed.

- Scandals within some industries and organisations has resulted in an over dependency on internal specialist departments. Risk is an example, where many employees are completing extensive risk analysis in preparation for responding to their colleagues like they would an external auditor. Organisations should consider building capabilities across their organisation rather than building a dependency on a department within it.

- In many cases, there has been a relaunch of the brand, vision, mission and values with a communication exercise to educate the workforce—most likely several times this century. It would be interesting to ask employees, within the organisation, how much it helped them with their role and the growth of the business. Would the expense and effort be better focused on driving differentiation through increasing your market and business?

'When you have twenty people who all share roughly the same educational and life experiences, they're going to come up with the same solutions to the same problems.'
—Robert Webb

Multiple generations within the workforce is an opportunity to generate a diverse range of thought. Many organisations engage multiple generations; however, does each generation iterate on the previous? Are we out of balance by wanting to integrate new thoughts from the generation entering the workforce? The world is now global, and we may need to consider those in other geographies. Organisations must now consider those countries that are part of the global world entering their market. Let's refer to these as 'entering global'. How do they incorporate more balance or even shift the thinking from generational to entering global? Teams should consist of individuals from diverse geographies.

The frantic nature of organisations today has impaired the quality of thought. Organisational thinking is either consciously or unconsciously biased based on the experiences of those within it. This frantic nature creates anxiety. Many, who now lead organisations, commenced their career pre internet and have seen unprecedented change during their career as the world entered the information age. People within organisations are impacted by the expectation of franticness, getting involved and 'leaning in'. There is a tendency by employees to increase the volume of their work and remain busy. This is one of several dimensions regarding the work within an organisation and its significance:

- What is the work people are doing? What is generating that work and what is its period of relevance?

- Why do people continue doing the work as it may have been done for a considerable period—not the technology they are using but their mindset? The technology could be contributing to the situation as it often helps keep up with the volume, enabling the continuance of less valuable work.

- Organisations have implemented Agile, Lean or Design Thinking and have created space for these activities; however, if they are still doing the same work in a new way, how much has really changed? For many organisations, the volume of work has remained but is being managed differently. The work in many instances remains unchallenged because mindset has not shifted. People have been trained in a new process but not in a new way of thinking. Is the work valuable? How could it be more valuable and what needs to stop?

- Organisations are wrestling with how to anticipate and beat an emerging start-up competitor. Organisations *create* a start-up space without *being* a start-up. People working in the space are unlikely to leave their permanent role for a start-up and they are studying start-ups that are beyond starting-up.

- The next start-up is not thinking about its space, digital tools or Agile scrum. They are likely firmly focused on an idea that involves winning your customers, building a digital ecosystem, and eroding your traditional business model. The majority of them are doing this without all the distractions of being within a large enterprise.

We are all potentially having the wrong conversation. Are large organisations focused on symptoms rather than the root of the opportunity? What is holding organisations back and what could the conversation be?

Now is the time to ask people to think about their work, what type of work it is and why it is occurring. Do this before considering digital. Specifically, what problems are they solving?

> 'Knowledge is of no value unless
> you put it into practice.'
> —Anton Chekhov

It's time for employees within organisations to consider if they should continue their work. Organisations need to help and reward their people for stopping the work. We have rewarded people for their output. Many organisations have identified highly skilled people who are great at getting work done and as a result, the amount of work, for many employees, has increased. Often employees within organisations seek to expand the work they undertake to demonstrate they are useful, a key contributor and a team player. However, this attitude is eroding the potential of the broader business as organisations become stuck in the business of today.

We now need to consider rewarding people for thought.

Further, every organisation has a group of employees who think differently. How big is this group within your organisation and what are they really doing? What is the guerrilla movement within your organisation? How can this be supported? There is an opportunity to discover and connect these people with the broader organisation; however, these people will probably not be motivated to take more work but they will be motivated by evolving the work. Many of these people within my career have assisted in incubating a shift of thinking and subsequent transitions within an organisation.

Organisations must align to the opportunity of thinking about the work and having a conversation regarding the value, rather than the volume, of work.

Assessing work

Prior to considering how digital may be part of your business, it's valuable to consider the work that is currently being undertaken to support the business. The work can be assessed.

There are four profiles within an assessment that offer insight into an organisation. It is likely there will be a dominant profile and an opportunity to shift for your organisation. I have developed a Pre-Digital Assessment framework for organisations to initiate their assessment of their work.

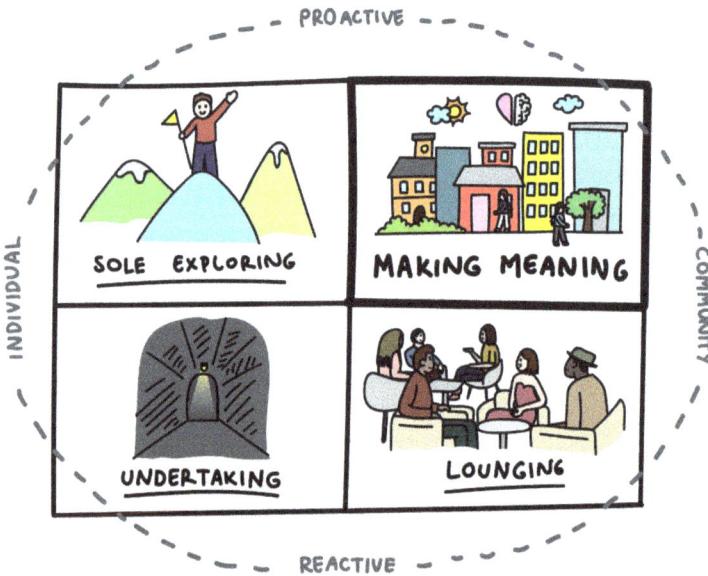

Figure 1: Pre-Digital Assessment (Affectionately referred to by my clients as PDA)

Undertaking (individual and reactive work)

These people simply do the work. They may have tried to change the work, but their concerns and ideas have been ignored or suppressed. Their work is not exciting and is sometimes complex. They have not had the regular opportunity or potentially don't have the inclination to evolve how the work is undertaken. There is little interest in how work is done until something goes wrong. When something does go wrong, people external to the work are surprised that people are still operating in this way. Although upon reflection they are not surprised, they are conflicted with how best to help address these situations. Further, in many of these situations the relationships between individuals doing the work and the market are distant, and interactions are infrequent and awkward. Consequently, if this continues, the organisation will become less competitive and will carry greater risks.

For those doing the work, there is a feeling of isolation. These people generally don't want to talk about the work as it is mundane and on occasions complex—nobody really understands it or would want to.

Basically, work is fragmented across the organisation and activities are being undertaken by a single person or a few people. In summary:

- Those doing the work consider it dire and inevitable (a little like death).
- The broader community is distracted by other things.
- Nobody wants to engage as there are other things of greater interest.

Lounging (community and reactive internal work)

This group is collectively comfortable; the business has been successful using a consistent approach. The organisation is a bit special—the people think so. People external to the organisation don't really understand us. Some practices have been refined internally; however, they are not comparable to other organisations, so we think. We tend to find rationales to not pursue things with greater urgency; people within our organisation are quick to agree with these rationales. The organisation has a strong identity and people are valued by fitting in with that identity. This sounds wonderful; however, it is potentially catastrophic as people first seek to fit in and be accepted. Social compliance rather than contribution is rewarded. It is dangerous to be a little different—remember those people who were a little different? I wonder where they are and what they are doing now.

This group of people (could be a team, department, organisation, community, country) is comfortable with its collective consensus:

- This is how we do things here: it's why we are different (a little bit special), just ask anyone here and they will tell you.

- We are open to new things; however, these things need to fit in with how things are done here.

- We talk about possibilities and options; however, this doesn't progress into action. Talk is good, and action is scary.

- We have thought about change but now is not the right time.

- Why would we upset everyone with doing something different?

Sole exploring (individual and proactive external work)

Sole explorers are externally focused and not connected internally. They are tripped up by others doing something similar. They are bright. They are internal disruptors but are often not thinking holistically or executing on an agreed set of priorities. They have a different speed. They have a black operations mentality of special projects; waste is being created.

This group is also fragmented. People are off doing what *they* think needs to be done (but often struggle to reconcile how their change can scale):

- There is a series of initiatives based on people's own preferences not linked to the bigger picture.

- People become frustrated; they disengage and choose to do what they want.

- People and teams are doing similar things but they are not connected or working together.

- Great efforts are made by people working in isolation; however, the outcome could have been phenomenal if others were involved.

- There are too many secrets, there is high competition and people plot against one another. People are quick to judge others and dismiss their thoughts; they believe they know better.

If any of the above three groups dominate an organisation, it is likely that the future potential of the business is not being realised. If this work continues, what would the future look like?

Making meaning (community and external proactive work)

This group has a greater sense of purpose; they feel proud to contribute to this being realised. There is a sense of selflessness and a willingness to help others before themselves. This is a community that can link beauty to engineering, humanity to technology and poetry to processes. (Isaacson, 2015)

People in this group are intellectually connected and emotionally invested.

- The bigger picture is clearly understood; the group regularly shares and assesses activity. They link their efforts to the bigger picture; they are selfless.

- Difficult decisions were made after appropriately engaging broader communities, including a global perspective.

- People take the time to listen, constructively challenge, and learn and share. This has shaped 'our work'.

- There is balance between internal views with perspectives from external communities making the work meaningful.

- They have integrated, and continue to strive to simplify work.

- They are connected yet respectfully challenge one another. They don't agree all the time, and this is a great source of ideas/creativity.

- People seek to learn rather than show what they know. There is no grandstanding, there is a humility that transcends through the organisation.

Making meaning is the future of work. It's how organisations can be globally aware and locally accountable.

Remediating the work

The four profiles of work present different opportunities to an organisation. There is temptation for executives to self-assess and commence remediation immediately. An approach of top down critical activities based on a burning platform or crisis may initially address some symptoms; however, this approach is unlikely to realise the potential of the employee's contribution to the business. The broader employees are key to shifting the organisation to realise its potential.

- Early employee involvement with the assessment, exploring remediation options and owning the shift will contribute to improving organisational knowledge of how work can be assessed.

- Developing the discipline of fewer meaningful actions based on the assessment.

- Creating a consciousness that will avert similar scenarios manifesting in the future.

- Lightening of the load and reducing risk as the right work, rather than all possible work, is progressed.

Generally, the preferred employees (to be involved with the shift) are management (not executives), team leaders and key contributors (known as the *core group*). It's important that those who will become initially involved can be a respected advocate to the broader employee population. This advocacy is to those within their department, across various other departments and upwards to the executives of the organisation. The core group's effort will be directly influenced by others through their openness and willingness. How can others successfully influence those sharing information? By initially listening and then considering how they can genuinely support the shift. This support will be different across organisations.

This core group of employees should begin by analysing the existing 'commitments'. 'Commitments' are time takers and erode the potential of what needs to be committed to. Sometimes they are the areas of limited value.

Responsibilities, Activities and Initiatives (RAI): redefining the work

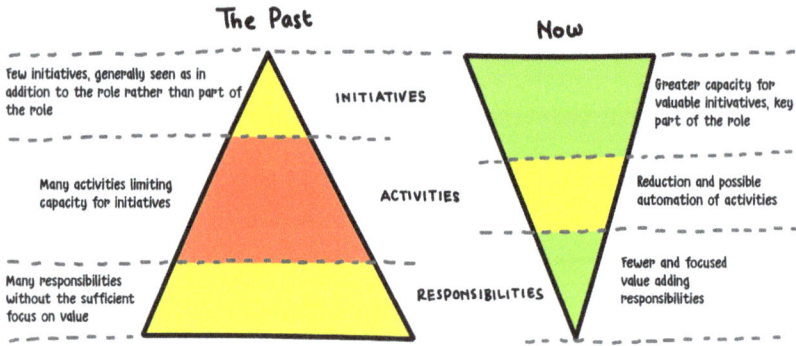

Figure 2: RAI

This core group of employees can become initially involved by using the RAI principle, which I developed.

Responsibilities

- What is expected of your role in the upcoming period?

- Review the existing list, challenge the items on it and endeavour to rationalise as many items as possible, transition from 'The Past' to 'Now'.

- Circulate an updated list upon completing the above. There will be people who will want to add items. You will need to consider if these are Responsibilities (R) or the AI in RAI. Generally, many of the suggestions will be Activities and Initiatives.

Activities

- What Activities are needed to support the Responsibility's initiation, ongoing commitment and completion? Note that the time commitment will vary potentially due to the stage the team is at (storming, forming, norming) and the experience and capabilities of those people within the team.

- There may be a desire to be involved in everything, to show your worth and possibly prove why you are valued. People need to consider avoiding this as it will consume the capacity created. It's also energy draining and can potentially alienate people.

- Identify the valuable Activities aligned to your Responsibilities. It's important to rationalise the Responsibilities to the items that are valuable and challenge legacy Activities.

- What are the Activities that will continue? How repeatable and predictable are they? Could they be automated?

Initiatives

- The more capacity you have for Initiatives, the greater the potential benefit for the broader organisation.

- An Initiative may be a dedicated team tasked with addressing an opportunity. This team may benefit from your presence at certain meetings (not all) or only require you to speak with its members occasionally. By doing this, you create scale and capacity.

When completed effectively, Responsibilities become very clear, Activities are reduced with some of those remaining being automated and the capacity for Initiatives increases. When the group completes the RAI activity, it will have identified areas that will require a shift from others. This core group of employees is like a fire starter: it's the spark in the kindling and it positively spreads to other employees. The other employees will want to become involved. Generally, many of these employees can see the benefit of reducing Activities that enable the capacity for Initiatives. The approach will vary across organisations but the objective will remain the same: for employees to start and continue to own their transition.

Below are examples of some shifts. Every organisation will identify varying shifts and the specific changes should not be prescribed but rather identified from within. Part of the growth of the organisation is learning through doing the work and specifically identifying the root of something rather than simply identifying the symptom.

Undertaking

- Congregate employees either physically or virtually.
- Eliminate non-value adding activities.
- Eliminate overlaps, rationalise and integrate work where possible.
- Consider automating the work that is value adding.

Lounging

- Educate the collective group.
- Remediation begins within the group with a concerted effort to move away from current thinking.
- Some role decisions may be required—consider realigning leadership and manager roles.
- Identify areas of hope: what is working well and how could this be replicated in other areas? Encourage people to share so others can adopt these practices.

Sole exploring

- Inform people of the work.

- Consider how to integrate the work into the bigger picture. This may by integrating similar Initiatives and groups of people.

- Stop the work that doesn't link to the bigger picture.

- Validate intent and progress: how could this work be truly phenomenal?

Making meaning

- Share across the organisation.

- Continue to replicate approach and grow one another.

- Educate broader communities.

- Continue to build the company's reputation with external communities.

- Identify what is not digital and decide if it could be digital. Create a schedule of what is going digital.

As already mentioned, there is a temptation for executives to self-remediate. Let me repeat: don't. Avoid prescribing the above list. The list can be used to inspire action from within teams; however, the shift or change is achieved by the participation of the community. The leadership group can initiate and support the change; however, the activity must be owned by the broader group. The alignment across the community is the first step in achieving a sustainable change. This alignment begins with the executive team, then the leadership teams and then the employee. This happens through:

1. Understanding the Pre-Digital Assessment method and potential.

2. Genuine acknowledgement of the opportunities likely to be presented through the assessment of the work.

3. Support to remediate the findings with a key group of employees leading by example with their RAI.

The benefits are beyond the initial changes of work. There is a change of thinking and greater thought given to future work. This will be the foundation for an organisation's digital potential. This is second order change.

At a leadership program of one of my employers, we discussed the different types of change and how to avoid the temptation of addressing symptoms. This was referred to as first order change. Second order change is far more sustainable than first order change. In applying first order change, the work is refined and improved. The change could be negative as non-value adding work continues. Second order change considers a deeper, more thoughtful approach. This change can be different to the efforts of the past as it encourages thinking and then remediation. (Watzlawick, Weakland, & Fisch, 1974)

Avoid the temptation of tinkering with the work by removing some of the complexity; seek to transition to less work that is more valuable. This is an important initial phase for establishing the foundations of a digital organisation.

Professional ignorance: dumb or numb?

The word ignorance is strong and when followed by dumb, it becomes amplified. As I stated earlier, there will be times where I use language to make a point. If you are tempted to skim over this section, I encourage you to reconsider as it is the foundation. Progress will be limited without people being involved; it will not be second order change.

'People's ignorance really pees me off. Stupidity is when you can't help it – Ignorance is when you choose not to understand something.'

—Sarah MacLachlan

Some organisations choose not to consider the work being undertaken within their organisation. They choose to ignore the complexity, potentially because it is a difficult topic—this is dumb. Other organisations that fail are likely to have many circumstances of poor judgement and poor work with systemic problems—this is more being numb. Another scenario could be that the breadth of work and pressure to complete the work have resulted in continued non-value adding work, and in a boxing sense, the organisation is on the ropes and change is inevitable.

Regardless of the circumstance, the likely probability is that these issues will be exacerbated within the digital world.

Digitally dumb

The digital world can simplify (through automation) but can also complicate. Organisations may miss the opportunity to rationalise the work prior to digitising the work. There is a probability that some organisations will be digitally dumb as they automate work that is no longer, or soon to be no longer, relevant. There are parallel learnings to be taken from organisations that have outsourced their work prior to simplifying the work. These outsourcing arrangements create the same mess, just with less costs. Often referred to as 'mess for less', a first order change.

There is an added layer between the source of the potential problem and those who choose to resolve it. As digital work is not physical work, the instances or frequency of the problem will be amplified. A simple example is hacking an enterprise system that results in the theft of electronic customer records where thousands of people are implicated compared with physically breaking into a home, which is traumatic but fewer people are implicated.

Digitally numb

There may be some organisations that assess their work, tinker with it but don't truly act on it. The quality of work will improve and the ability to compete in a digital world may be extended; however, this is not existing in a digital world. It is likely that over time, these organisations will diverge from their potential and become less relevant to their customers.

Both situations are different but originate from ignorance.

Resistance

Change can elicit a range of responses from people but there are two types of resistance that those initiating the change are likely to encounter.

Active resistance is when a person or group will openly challenge something. The challenging behaviour offers the opportunity to understand and potentially resolve the areas of concern. With active resistance, you know what you are dealing with.

Passive resistance is unknown and can remain unknown for a considerable period. You don't know what you are dealing with; however, you know something is not right. There is an inkling and it needs to be dealt with.

Both will require the alignment of teams. Great teams with a shared outcome will have more constructive conflict. It will be uncomfortable on occasions but this uncomfortable feeling should not erode people's contribution. When it does, people become complacent; they sit it out when they are expected to be involved. Aligning teams to a shared outcome is paramount to achieving the outcomes. If this is not in place, potential is unrealised.

Aligning teams

We can expect to face varied and unpredictable responses from people when change is introduced. There exists a very sensible leadership approach to setting expectations to how leaders can best help their teams through this period. Some of these practices were introduced to me over a decade ago (others more recently); they have proven to be consistently practical for the teams I have worked with ever since.

> 'A leader is best when people barely know he exists, when his work is done, his aim fulfilled, they will say: we did it ourselves.'
> —Lao Tzu

After any change within an organisation, there will be a period of resettling and resetting. It is during periods of change that things are tested, and this is the time when leadership is the difference. The appropriate leadership, at the time, helps people through this transition. Leaders should embody a spirit of being approachable and available (not absent) but should also avoid being 'all over everything'.

Be the *lighthouse*

This means maintaining consistency and visibility, being yourself, and being there when people need you. A lighthouse is visible in the storm; it is there in the distance but can be easily found when people travel too close to the rocks. The lighthouse doesn't seek to dominate or cast its light everywhere—that is the purpose of the light bulb. People sometimes confuse the light bulb with the lighthouse: light bulbs flood rooms with light, causing the light from others to be lost.

Remind people of the difference between the lighthouse and light bulb. When something is important (like one's work), there is a tendency for some people to act, albeit with good intentions, and flood others with their light, which may drive them into the shadows and fracture the team.

Stay *on the balcony*

Seek to understand rather than be understood. When leaders talk to people, they take the time to listen and reflect. Opinions are everywhere; whereas, understanding is not. It's easier in this time of information overload to respond quickly and move on, but this will not build the foundations of a solid relationship. Imagine sitting on a balcony on a warm, breezy evening (everything seems a little clearer when you do). Be considered in your responses, frugal with your words and create an environment that can be filled with thoughts from others.

Seeking to align an understanding of the above starts with those who report to you (the people you serve). However, the purpose of this exercise is not to align thinking but to align behaviour and language. Through aligning the latter, the former can be shared: diversity of thought is the beginning of creativity. Sharing thoughts has many benefits beyond creativity in that it establishes an environment of openness and sharing.

'Transitions should be constant'; they help avert the need for transformation

Many organisations lurch from one transformation to another; often, there is a burning platform that creates the need for transformation. Metaphorically speaking, this platform sometimes started as a discarded match or an ember drifting from a poorly managed campfire. When asked about the burning platform, people had been aware of it; they had talked about it among themselves, sometimes for a considerable period of time, but little was done and so the problem grew over time. Organisations today need to know that there are many floating embers and that management is not always in the best position to see them or to know when and where they will land—but their people will know.

Those in leadership positions must emphasise to the broader community that they are likely to see things that are occurring within the organisation prior to those leading the organisation. The leaders may see some symptoms however somebody within the organisation is likely to know why something is occurring; the source. The ember that has landed and initiated a spot fire.

'Building alignment vertically' within organisations is undervalued

Leadership teams can spend a great deal of time and energy aligning their organisation horizontally, with their peers or their direct reports. While this is important, there needs to be a balance. Executives can become frustrated with and confused by the engagement within their organisation. Year after year, they will review their employees' engagement scores and be surprised at the lack of appreciation for their efforts at horizontal alignment.

Leaders need to spend more time within their organisation 'talking with' people rather than 'at them'. They need to be involving rather than interfering or interrogating. I have seen both in many organisations and when this occurs, information flows reduce.

'Talking with' people

Conversations are often started with a perspective. Within organisations, this is generally due to somebody caring about something, wanting to share something or being confused about something. The things people think about are influenced by their inputs. Many executives don't dedicate time to regularly sharing their thoughts. They will share the status of certain activities, but there is a reluctance to share their thought processes. Perspectives are important to people; they want to know what their leaders are thinking and this thinking is a key input.

Blogging is not common enough within organisations: 'blogs share perspectives'

There are many corporate communications: weekly updates, new intranet articles and corporate social media interactions, all of which create a general sense of awareness but may never convey a sense of who somebody is. Why? These communications are written by someone else for somebody else; it's the core of somebody else's thinking, and people can tell.

Blogs, however, can help create understanding. To do this, a good blog should consist of:

- A weekly recognition of effort by the team that is aligned with the broader strategic direction. Avoid building a hero culture by calling out extraordinary efforts by an individual. Doing so can alienate team members.

- An external story of interest related to the industry with some insight for the organisation or what you are now going to do differently.

- A personal insight. This can be from your week at work, something from your personal life or a recollection from your career. It's ok to be yourself and to be different; this insight should allow people to get to know you better so that when they meet you in person, there will be familiarity and a place to start a conversation.

- Finally, the blog should be published at the same time every week. A former colleague once said that she could almost set her watch by the publication of my blog.

These blogs can be supported by a vlog (a message from a leader delivered by video); however, blogs remain important and a vlog supports the blog rather than it being a substitute. Blogs can be printed and put on a wall, they can be saved and referred to in the future—like a book that can be endured.

'Sharing experiences' as a team

There are meetings and then there are off sites. While most of us have attended many, how often are they remembered as an experience that shifted the group? People tend to recall the bad, including those with pointless activities and long lists of flip-chart actions. Those actions are tracked and completed, but they don't create a shift. Some of the best experiences are when conversations address the potential of a situation and a shared understanding is developed.

> 'A lot of why I climb is for the friendship, the loyalty, the shared experience of being in that moment.'
> —Jimmy Chin

Further, these conversations and experiences have a ripple effect. Once the team finds its rhythm, team members generally want to involve others in the experience, often including their management and key influencers. Do this! This is when vertical alignment is genuinely achieved. Sometimes, people don't even realise they're in vertical alignment until the leadership changes or reverts to former practices.

Mindset recap

Here is a summary of the key components:

- A **growth mindset** will set the right conditions of learning and openness.

- Current **work is not the future**, assessment is required, and **remediation is possible** by applying RAI.

- Probability of **professional ignorance** increases in uncharted waters. Check if you are being digitally dumb or numb.

- Expect resistance and be prepared to **align teams** and have teams **share experiences.**

- Your personal leadership is likely to be a combination of the **lighthouse**; staying on the **balcony** during some conversations; **talking with** rather than **at** people; and being prepared to **blog and share perspectives.**

PART 2

TECHNOLOGY

Lifting the mystique and taking off the technology handbrake

If you are reading this section, you have made it beyond *Your Mindset* and are open to digital possibilities—this is very exciting. Technology is the core topic here; however, transparency is at the essence and will be carried through this section.

Technology can and should be an enabler yet some believe it slows the possibility of an organisation realising its potential. In effect, it's a handbrake.

This section has a key dependency on the technology team within an organisation including:

- Transparency of costs, and how priorities can be communicated simply.
- What to do if there is not a technology strategy.
- How to remain actively engaged with the business.
- The opportunity that better understanding processes presents for people in organisations.

Transparency

The intersect of 'technology' and 'digital' today presents the greatest opportunity for a mainstream technology executive and her/his team more than at any other time in history. This is not something that people can leap into but it is something that technology executives will be key contributors to.

'We believe that transparency is needed to create trust, and it's also needed to create dialogue.'

—Julie Sweet

As the organisation matures with a series of digital initiatives, there will be a need for greater communication of technical topics. This practice should start now. There will be a need to communicate regularly and without complexity; therefore, it is important that the fundamentals of technology are well managed and understood. Establishing and maintaining the basics with regular progress and communication—without the geek speak—is the first step.

Here are some of the key areas that require transparency.

1. Costs

When technology budgets are broken down by department and service, the numbers become blurred. Instead, set out to rank costs from the highest to the least expensive (1–10 or 1–20) and include commentaries relating to when each item was last reviewed, ideally with a benchmark, or is to be reviewed (e.g. through an activity like a vendor negotiation). Use the approach to run and change budgets in separate tables.

Include total labour as a separate line item. What is the outlook? For example, technology labour costs for a regular technology function are expected to reduce as automation opportunities increase. Don't shy away from this; if it's not included, it will soon be introduced by somebody else. The titles and descriptions within all organisations will vary; however, here is an example.

Top budget items	Millions $	% of budget	Comments
Salary (FTE and contractors)	4.7	39%	Ongoing reductions expected with implementation of IAAS.
Infrastructure/ Cloud Infrastructure	2.5	21%	Internal infrastructure is below market for IAAS. Migration to occur at end of life.
Network	1.2	10%	Costs benchmarked annually.
ERP (two key systems)	1.5	13%	Opportunity for consolidation. If a single system is selected avoid customisation to allow portability in the future.
Office software	0.8	7%	Three-year term at benchmark.
Other applications	0.4	3%	Some to be reduced due to security vulnerabilities and negligible financial benefit.
Specialist software	0.3	3%	Agreed with key business representatives.
Partners/ Consultants	0.3	3%	
Many miscellaneous costs	0.3	3%	
Note: laptop, print and mobile costs are passed through to the business.			*Costs are benchmarked annually within current contracts.*
Total	**12**		

Table 1: Technology costs breakout example (note % have been rounded up)

On some occasions, budgets may be held outside of the technology area and may be managed differently to the above. Regardless of how these budgets are managed, apply the level of rigour outlined above (your rows may be different). I have applied this approach to several million dollar, 10-million dollar and 500-million dollar budgets. Larger budgets will have more lines; I have had up to 20+ lines for larger budgets. Adopting this approach will demonstrate the benefits of simplifying information to the organisation. It will allow others to consider if they replicate it and it will allow the organisation to look at synergies of activities. It is likely there will be synergies between the digital and technology spend.

Areas of future investment will require funding from somewhere. Sometimes, funding can be achieved through efficiencies across an organisation.

2. Capability and outcomes are multiplied by mentoring

What is the number and percentage of people working within various parts of the organisation? What were the numbers twelve months ago, and what will the numbers be in twelve months from now? As an example, the resources engaged by the technology team in the domain of 'infrastructure' (e.g. data centres and servers) should be declining and those in emerging domains (e.g. data science) could be increasing.

> 'Technology's great, but you can only be as good in technology as your people are.'
>
> —Gillian Tans

Percentages are important for areas with few people but use both numbers and percentages. Below is a conceptual example.

Area	This year		Next year		Comments
Service desk	5	31%	4	24%	Site consolidation has enabled reduction.
Infrastructure	4	25%	2	12%	Reduction due to IAAS adoption.
Applications	2	13%	3	18%	Integration of specialist business systems person.
Management	2	13%	2	12%	No change.
Data	1	6%	3	18%	Two new data science roles.
Network	1	6%	2	12%	Required due to 24-hour operation and will add some further security capability.
Security	1	6%	1	6%	No change, new network resource is to support current resource.
	16		17		

Table 2: Technology human resources breakout
example (note % have been rounded up)

What are the resource bottlenecks to achieving outcomes? What has been addressed and what is in progress? Additionally, how is the talent within traditional services being transitioned into the emerging capability required? There are many people within organisations who align culturally and are intellectually capable, but they are not mentored appropriately. Good mentoring offers insight into how somebody could be an even greater contributor in the future.

Consider providing your leaders with mentoring training. Enable and encourage them to have regular, meaningful conversations with talented people across the organisation (which should go beyond their direct reports). Once these conversations occur, people generally think more and make more meaningful choices about what they would like to learn and do next. A person's choice will be the greatest motivator to the learning offered and how their skills will be applied. When these skills are applied in the right areas, positive outcomes increase.

3. Criticality

What is the list of initiatives (beyond BAU)? What are the business priorities? These priorities might not be projects; they could be the significant amount of work added to an Agile team's backlog.

Avoid immediately committing to undertaking these priorities as they arise. Stack rank them based on a sensible range of business criteria and make this process visible both physically and digitally. Openly share these priorities across the organisation, allow people to review and contribute, and invite debate. This list is dynamic. Maintaining the list should be the responsibility of a single person or a small group.

In establishing this process, things may initially slow down but it will ultimately allow them to go faster. Further, some initiatives may be potentially stopped. Prior to stopping anything, consider the following:

- *Accelerate things that are two-thirds complete (consider yourself an air traffic controller clearing the skies).*

- *For those that remain, look for opportunities to integrate initiatives. It's surprising how many times you will have a similar request from different areas.*

- *Regarding the things that you may need to stop, be open and communicate the points made above and list the more pressing initiatives. When people understand that rigour has been applied to possible initiatives, they tend to accept what is best for the organisation.*

4. Communicate consistently with context

Transparency builds trust and then empathy; these are important foundations for the future. Technology executives can lead by example. Avoid seeking understanding and empathy when there is no transparency. This is likely to be a credibility killer.

Reflect upon what is being made visible across your organisation. Is this information—as 6pt font line items in an Excel spreadsheet—showing availability? Is there any commentary offered? Is this information easily accessible? How regularly is it shared? Does this information reconcile with other functions, data and perspectives? Is there alignment and debate invited where previously this was not the case? This debate will be important if you are to realise your potential. Diversity of thought contributes to innovation.

Are you communicating by exception? Technology executives take note: beyond the operational metrics generally available within any good technology function, you must share information on costs and capabilities regularly and this should come with commentary. Insights shared across an organisation build trust and allow people to consider practical and meaningful actions.

Be open and prepared to talk about everything—what's gone well and what hasn't. By taking the time to offer commentary on the numbers, actions being undertaken and expected results, there is transparency and the opportunity for understanding. This understanding will enable greater connections, which will be important for future efforts.

Tech strategy-less

Sometimes, due to unforeseen circumstances, there may not be a feasible or current strategy in place. There are many potential reasons for this, and here is a possible scenario: you have joined an organisation that was recently acquired and you have stepped into an acting role as CIO. The technology team needs to evolve rapidly because the business is booming, the strategy has lapsed and, due to several more pressing priorities, is unable to be renewed at this time.

> 'Stone Age. Bronze Age. Iron Age.
> We define entire epics of humanity
> by the technology they use.'
> —Reed Hastings

Many years ago, one of my roles allowed me to work with and visit many CIOs, heads of IT and other technology executives. It was interesting to discuss what they were doing when there was no strategy. CIOs are often referred to as *the core system lady, the chap that built our software development capability* or *the cloud guy*. They become defined by their major initiative. Sometimes, the initiative is not something they have chosen; instead, it is initiated due to the circumstances. The very effective leader can span beyond this and here is what I learned from them.

What should the technology team do?

- Accept that there will be an expectation of thought and action, ideally simultaneously, from the broader organisation.

- It is likely that conversations within the organisation will shift from the work at hand to speculation on what's next and that people will fill the void if there is limited direction—be prepared to hear this third-hand.

- There could be some fraying and fragmentation of the technology team as it creates its own meaning. Identify areas that may break away or dig in and reach out to those teams early on.

- There will be a heightened risk of losing key personnel due to uncertainties, so review your talent and key-person grid. Leaders should commence scheduling 30-minute conversations with these people as soon as possible.

- People will look more critically at their leaders. You can expect them to try and read your body language and the nuances in what is being said. Leaders accept this and adopt a mindset of being the 'lighthouse in the storm'. Remain genuine, sincere, balanced and with a positive outlook. Avoid the danger of being insincere. People will recall what is said or not said at this time, and when done well, it will result in trust.

In all of these scenarios, there are three common areas that can create focus and serve the business, the organisation and the technology team. The organisations I visited had subtleties within their organisational language regarding their priorities; however, here are the consistent themes.

1. Fundamentals first (40 to 60% of your focus)

A global CIO at one of my former employers once said that we would not keep our jobs only by ensuring that the network and emails were performing; instead, we would lose them quickly and if they failed, we would lose them almost instantly. This statement has stayed with me. In addition to this, here are some fundamentals for reviewing the key domains of your technology department and actions:

- Infrastructure or cloud-based (IAAS) technologies: Review the performance and capacity of these services in addition to any projects at hand. Consider what needs to be prioritised in order to ensure performance continues and capacity is not exceeded. While undertaking this, check for disaster recovery capability and history, as answers may indicate a priority in need of addressing this.

- Network: Failing or flaky networks dramatically impact on the employee experience, so identify the key partners in providing this service. Ask for their assistance in analysing the performance of the network and the areas in which capacity thresholds may be close to being reached (or, on occasion, exceeded) and prioritise resources to resolve this immediately.

- Applications: Are there any licensing arrangements due for renewal? Ideally, these should be in a single list. If not, start the list and let everybody know about it. Internally developed applications should be closely scrutinised by security professionals (more on security later).

- Data/management information: What is being used for reporting purposes? Ensure that key resources in this process are directly engaged and make the leaders available to them as an immediate escalation point.

- Security: How impartial is the team's reporting line? If the Chief Information Security Officer, or equivalent, is not reporting to the CIO, make this change immediately. Ask what the outstanding backlog is and consider assisting the team by appointing an external professional security organisation for a period of time (avoid outsourcing this capability). Review their schedule of work and consider directing the team to areas of greatest vulnerability rather than sticking to the schedule developed over the last 12 to 24 months. In addition, directly engage the team and make yourself available to them as an immediate escalation point.

- Auxiliary functions: These could include the strategy, procurement, process, and project management teams. Seek to understand who these teams are interacting with and ensure that their services are maintained. These teams may feel vulnerable at this time, given that you are taking a deeper dive into the technology team—so look to how these teams can help with the review and the other two areas.

2. Simplify (30 to 40% of your focus)

It is likely that demand will either be restated to you or be increased as anxiety within the broader organisation increases (due to some of the reasons listed earlier). There are several areas that should be simplified:

- Capturing and reviewing demand: If there isn't a process, establish one, as well as some criteria for assessing this demand. The criteria should be aligned with the broader organisational strategy.

- At every organisation (excluding those as a management consultant) I have worked for this century (five different organisations in four different industries across various continents), there have been more active projects than the team could possibly deliver within the desired time frames. Review these initiatives (they could be a project or a significant effort added to an Agile team's backlog). Often, these projects are not as critical as some of the fundamental activities listed above. Be mindful of this as resources are balanced across initiatives.

- While analysing demand, consider what initiatives, technologies and mindsets may be fragmenting the technology landscape and identify opportunities for consolidation. There will be occasions in which technologies will not be consolidated due to maintaining or introducing some competitive tension—the technology team is to be informed of these situations.

- Analyse processes prior to coding: Simplify processes and aim to only agree to prioritising initiatives that align with key organisational processes.

The *Fundamentals first* and *Simplify* focuses will need to be supported with a simple engagement approach by the technology team, which is included later in this section.

3. Enable innovation (10 to 20% of your focus)

There is a risk that the first two activities will limit the broader potential value of the technology team's strategic contribution. It is likely that there are innovation initiatives underway, so be careful of several factors:

- Implementing Design Thinking, Lean and Agile is not innovation. While such an approach could assist with delivering innovation, it is not a source of innovation.

- Involve your partners in the conversation early. In addition, seek to experiment with partners who are willing to understand your business first and align relevant areas of innovation to be of value to your business.

- Be mindful of technology organisations' innovation agendas—they are often driven by good marketing intended to increase the sales of a certain service. With global technology organisations, seek to align with a global sponsor that should first seek to understand your business and may introduce you to similar organisations that are non-competing in other geographies.

- Successful innovation is not driven or owned by technology departments—it's enabled through them in partnership with the business and possibly other external parties. Involve others early as innovation options are explored.

- Consider your organisation's value chain and where greater value could be realised. For example, at a former employer, the pre-delivery and post-delivery stages offered greater potential for innovation. Such areas should be identified and explored with partners.

Finally, the tactics outlined above should not be a substitute for a broader technology strategy. While operating within these three areas of focus, the technology team's knowledge will be improved. This knowledge will contribute to the creation of a relevant, meaningful technology strategy at the appropriate time.

Remaining actively engaged

There is a chance that after engaging the broader organisation with the reinvigorated strategy and agreed priorities, the technology team will put its head down and get on with things without being actively engaged. The technology team may do this as it is stretched and is choosing to interact based on the initiatives underway. This is not sustainable.

> 'Relationships feed on credibility,
> honesty and consistency.'
> —Scott Borchetta

Technology teams are now interacting in a more meaningful manner. Many are moving from a service provider mentality to a business partner mentality seeking to create value. This has increased over the last five or so years, for a range of reasons like technology being integrated into customer offerings. Also, there is a broader interest from the business in how technology teams get their work done (i.e. Agile) and in the growing greater dependence on their technical expertise for a range of emerging business needs such as digital business activities, operations automation, smart technologies, etc.

Furthermore, the technology team must explain to fellow executives how technology works within the organisation without the complexity and detail. This could be during a conversation in a lift, some context setting within a board meeting, directing a project sponsoring executives' thinking to a certain area within a wider context, and general executive interaction within a meeting offering an update to explain what the team is working on today. There is a simple analogy that works with non-technical executives, which includes a modern twist about a 'house'.

Figure 3: Information technology house

The 'house' analogy

- The foundation of the house is the **Infrastructure**: the data centre and servers. These are now being replaced by cloud-based services. Roles are reducing in this area of the technology team as the work is moved to the cloud and then automated. You are not able to see the foundations; however, you know when they are unstable as the experience is poor (i.e. the house needs restumping as the floor/**Infrastructure** becomes unstable).

- The frame of the house is the **Network**, which intersects with the foundation and allows people to move within the house. Without the frame/**Network**, the house collapses.

- The door and windows offer access to **Applications**. Some will have different protocols for access. Just like a house, you can enter some rooms through an open door or perhaps by having a key. Some doors may be hidden and only known by those who use them.

- Furnishings within the rooms may be fixed and some other pieces allow you to interact with them, like **Data** or a **Mobile Application**. This interaction enables access to **Data** when you are in a room of the house. In some instances, you may only be able to view the furnishings/**Data** through a window provided by others (e.g. reporting). Also, some of the furniture is portable: you take it out on the lawn, down the street and this allows you to enjoy a lighter experience (e.g. **Mobile Application**).

- The fence around the house is the **Security**. This fence has been extended and has gained height over recent times. It is now more like a 'bubble' around the property. This bubble is constantly being monitored and is more dynamic than other parts of the house.

The analogy simply explains the components and interdependencies of the technology within an organisation. It can also assist in investment prioritisation conversations regarding the importance of foundations as solid with an appropriate reaching network, and the need to keep everything safe.

There is a very common scenario within all organisations today, where colleagues not working in or with the technology team want to deploy software as a service application. Colleagues will seek to avoid placing an application on the foundations or across the network, which is commonly known as a 'shadow application'. In many circumstances, this is technologically possible. However, the security position is almost always the stumbling block in how the shadow application can be provisioned for true enterprise use, and there are many reasons for this (e.g. data gathering, data access, secure user access).

Those working on security need to maintain their bubble, and if not already established, a *security as service* should be introduced. This is the rationale for why the Chief Information Security Officer or equivalent must report directly to the CIO. Beyond this, there will be future scenarios that are different, like shadow application scenarios with emerging digital capabilities aspired by organisations. It is likely there will be circumstances where digital capabilities will be implemented in a shadow scenario.

Expectations of the technology team to contribute to future digital business models and demand for resources will continue to increase. Beyond the interest of the working practices of the technology team, there is a growing interest in the technology capability of certain individuals within the team and how this capability could be applied to digital. This demand will stretch resources and potentially have consequences that need to be considered. Trade-off decisions are likely.

The technology team will need to inform the organisation of technical readiness with references to the technology within the organisation while integrating the digital future of an organisation. There will be a need to manage this demand and show progress. However, beyond this there needs to be a simple way to show progress and priorities. The DART assessment below can assist with this.

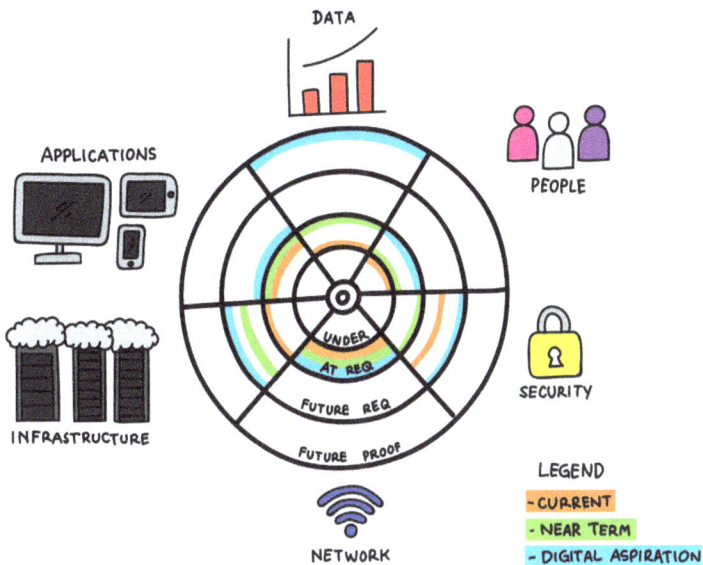

Figure 4: Digital Aspirations Readiness of Technology (DART) assessment

The DART assessment is not a strategic plan, it is an assessment of capability. Specifically, the DART assessment is used to show:

- Current capability. This is what your technology team is capable of with the technology that is currently available.

- Near-term capability. This is what the technology team is now working on (this could be a project or new release of an item in the Agile backlog) that will uplift current capability. This will benefit the organisation; however, it may not extend to the digital capabilities required.

- Digital demand that is dependent on the technology capability. The organisation has clearly articulated the digital strategy and plan. This plan has translated into technical requirements.

Establishing the Readiness of Technology is good practice. Including the Digital Aspirations may be optional for some organisations at this stage; however, the technology team needs to consider how to incorporate this demand at some stage. It is inevitable that digital will drive demand on all organisations.

Process and introverts

People, process and technology is a mantra used at an earlier time in the technology industry.

I have written much about the importance of people. I am a resolute believer that organisations have idle capability within them; those in leadership positions 'talk at people' rather than 'with people'. By being talked at, people will revert to someone else's expectations and their potential contribution will be unrealised. By 'talking with' people, a shared understanding is developed, and choices can be made, which are highly likely to include some discretionary effort from people. Choice is the greatest personal motivator.

> 'If you ask an introvert a question, wait until she thinks about it. Introverts think before speaking. If you want to get to the good stuff, you need to slow down.'
>
> —Laurie Helgoe

Sometimes it's difficult to have people open up about something. As a middle-aged man with middle-aged male friends, there are some parallels to how men consider and approach counselling. Some men find it difficult to see a counsellor; however, working together in a men's shed has proved successful in developing social support and camaraderie for men. In this regard, men who are marginalised and isolated have benefited from this very important initiative by working 'shoulder to shoulder' with others. Organisations can learn from this, in particular technology teams, where there are many clever and potentially intellectually idle people.

Many who work within the technology industry are introverts; thus, their thoughts are often not shared and are left unsaid in environments in which they are 'talked at'. Based on my personal experience over several decades at various organisations in different parts of the world, the thoughts from the introverted community are generally well developed as they have been thoroughly thought through prior to being shared.

Talking with people about 'processes' is a way to create an environment of working shoulder to shoulder with everyone and inviting everyone to participate. There is a methodology that can be utilised to engage these groups. Six Sigma developed a structured approach known as DMAIC for analysing and refining processes.[1,2] During the 1990s and early 2000s, there was a very strong positioning from those within organisations that were certified/accredited in Six Sigma: The approach is outlined below:

Define

- What is the problem?
- What is the scope?
- What key metric is important?
- Who are the stakeholders?

Measure

- What data is available?
- Is the data accurate?

Analyse

- What are the root causes of the problem?
- Have the root causes been verified?
- Where should the effort be focused?

Improve

- What are the possible solutions?
- How can the solutions be piloted?
- What were the results of the pilot?
- How can variances be reduced?

Control

- What is the preferred solution?
- What is the broader support for this solution?
- How can this solution be implemented?

In some organisations, these people became a group of fanatics endeavouring to grow their congregation with almost a religious zeal. In some instances, their evangelism alienated broader populations, and the good practices of sensible process analysis subsided. Interestingly, at present, the practice of Agile is the latest movement potentially being overplayed.

Process is the new black, but why and how?

Organisations are now able to reach customers anywhere; access is no longer the challenge and businesses don't have to open an office in a new location to enter a market. Additionally, a customer can choose when and where they would like to transact. The ease of customer interactions and transactions is paramount for any business.

Consider applying DMAIC with the objective of being closer to your customers:

- Moving closer to the end customer is the scope of the problem. (Define)

- What customer data is available across your industry or within your organisation? (Measure)

- What is distancing the relationship with the customer? (Analyse)

- What are the solutions that can be piloted and their results? (Measure)

Further, there is another structured approach within Six Sigma called SIPOC that can help move from supplier models to digital ecosystems:

- Supplier: Organisation that provides an input to a process.

- Input: What inputs are needed? What triggers an action?

- Policies: What policies, rules or regulations are in place?

- Outputs: What do your customers need?

- Customers: Who are your customers?

SIPOC can analyse existing suppliers and isolate what is needed in order to move to a digital ecosystem through breaking down components. Several former colleagues preferred an alternative approach to SIPOC as it was not customer centric. By starting with the customer, they revolutionised the process. Their thinking was SIPOC offered the current thinking paradigm. This was achieved by reversing SIPOC to COPIS (like others had) and began the analysis with the customer. COPIS eliminated waste, redefined thinking to the customer rather than the existing value chain and, in some instances, redefined supplier relationships or removed suppliers completely (which would enable a digital ecosystem).

> 'The most important single thing is to focus obsessively on the customer. Our goal is to be earth's most customer-centric company.'
>
> —Jeff Bezos

DMAIC and COPIS could contribute to an organisation implementing a digital business model. However, there are also broader benefits. At several organisations, I have literally observed those who have said very little in many meetings get out of their chairs in order to correct and add valuable insights (as people worked shoulder to shoulder using these models).

This is a practical approach to talking 'with' rather than 'at' people while shifting their digital contribution.

Technology recap

A brief summary of key topics:

- Strive to **be transparent** of the technology costs and capability. **Encourage mentoring** as it contributes to greater outcomes, **critically analyse initiatives, communicate** consistently and **provide context with any data.**

- If there is **no current technology strategy**, create **focus on** three areas: **fundamentals, simplify** and **enable innovation.**

- Remain **actively engaged** beyond the initial and regular communications, and **perfect the 30-second pitch** by explaining technology with a house analogy. Use DART to **explain initiatives creating uplifts.**

- Technology teams have introverts and techniques to **actively involve people.** Processes offer this opportunity.

PART 3

RELEVANCE

Sustaining transitions

Poor risk management capability will slow and potentially destroy an organisation's potential. Risk capability residing within teams who proactively apply this will help contribute to an organisation's relevance. Relevance is achieved through being in a state of constant transition. If risk management practices are not mature and across the employee population, activities will slow or stop.

Further, there is and will continue to be the need for organisations and particularly technology teams to right-size. There are a range of rationales including but not limited to automation, integration and rationalisation of roles. Many organisations take a phased approach to making these changes, eroding the contribution of the organisation due to 'interim organisations', and poorly led change.

Team alignment during this period of change requires an appropriate style of leadership, remaining visible and being willing to listen. This is 'vertically aligning' the organisation. Employee involvement post-transition reduces the dip in performance and can increase engagement when appropriately implemented.

Career management is paramount for any employee today. Remaining static in a dynamic world reduces the potential of contribution of anybody. Employees need to consider their professional capability and passion that can be dynamically shared with broader communities. Employees should be encouraged to proactively manage their career and ensure they remain current; this currency also translates into organisational relevance. Organisations will need to support their employees by growing their relevance; their retention will not be achieved by suppression but by the employees choosing the organisation.

Finally, leadership by the executive within their organisation and those first team leaders needs to be connected and empowering with eye cast outside of the organisation, with anticipation of what could be next and how the business remains relevant.

This section discusses the 'in between' area, the R in D-I-**R**-T-Y, the piece that links the foundations and exciting future possibilities:

- How to scale the risk capability across the employee population.

- The right size for the organisation and what opportunities will add capability.

- How to actively manage your career and encourage employees to do so too.

- How to create an experience where employees remain at your organisation.

- How to lead with greater relevance. Learnings from others that can make you more relevant.

Risk

This is a discipline to master in order to avoid your hands being the wrong type of dirty.

The professional services industry and internal risk functions within organisations have both grown considerably this century. There is a level of art and science within the practice of risk, and risk capability is something everyone within your organisation should have today as it will be important tomorrow.

The previous sections have reflected upon a learning mindset and transparency, which are important building blocks that, when applied consistently, ultimately create trust. However, trust can be easily lost when people are inconsistent. In this regard, consistent risk management practices through building capability, and keeping this at the front of one's mind and the regular discipline of action, will build on the trust established.

A greater number of employees with risk capabilities will increase the delivery velocity of initiatives, making for greater relevance of the organisation.

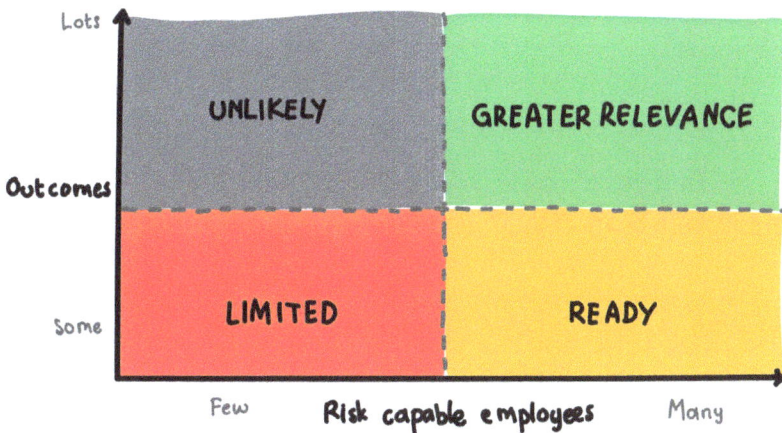

Figure 5: Relevance through risk chart

The risk that technology presents in organisations is considerable and the consequences are potentially catastrophic. The new ways in which people are working within organisations also present risk. A balance needs to be struck between new practices and the discipline of ensuring that risks are appropriately managed. When implemented appropriately, practices like Agile can assist with the management of risks.

There is and will continue to be a greater expectation and involvement of all professionals understanding and applying mature risk practices. Here is the science:

- Inherent risk: How 'likely' or 'bad' could this be?

- Residual risk: What are you comfortable tolerating? Accepting this risk needs to be within an organisation's appetite for risk.

How to strategically manage risk?

Controls are how you can minimise the likelihood and impact of the 'bad' thing occurring. There are several types of control:

- Preventative controls are best; however, they are not always available or possible. An example would be the encryption of data across a network within an Infrastructure as a Service.

- Detective controls can help minimise the event by identifying and actioning the event early in its occurrence. An example would be the deployment of a monitoring solution that would identify an extraction of data by a third party where encryption is not available across a network of an Infrastructure as a Service.

Who can implement controls?

- Primary controls can be implemented directly by the service provider (e.g. a large technology vendor would be ideal) or by the team managing the service (i.e. the application team).

- Leveraged controls are provided by another party (e.g. security with an organisation) and assist the team that is providing the service (i.e. the application team).

- Compensating controls are implemented by a team to manage risk prior to a primary or leveraged control being implemented. This situation is not ideal but is likely to assist in reducing inherent risk or possibly achieving a residual risk position.

How to manage issues?

Teams who analyse risks and implement controls will improve awareness and practices of risk. As the exercise is undertaken, it is likely there will be an identification of 'issues'. This is to be encouraged. An issue is an event—a 'bad' thing that has occurred.

- Teams should always be encouraged to self-identify issues.

- Issues should be documented with a forecasted closure date. If possible, expedite closure prior to the forecasted date.

- Teams should also be measured on both the frequency and length of issue extension rates. An issue not closing on the forecasted date may indicate an area of underinvestment or poor vendor performance.

Here are some insights into the art of risk and how you can encourage a risk culture beyond training, incentives and consequences:

- Encourage everyday awareness at every gathering: Introduce a risk moment at the beginning of team gatherings (e.g. someone can share a risk story or perspective). Civil construction organisations do this for safety; thus, increasing awareness and creating a safety mindset.

- Use Agile practices to assist risk management: Scrums and Visual Management Boards (VMBs) are effective ways of creating focus and demonstrating progress. Ensure minutes are maintained for these meetings.

- Place risk VMBs on the wall in a working area so they are an everyday reminder for people.

- Promote risk knowledge exchange by encouraging teams to visit another's Scrum, VMB and risk document portal. Be transparent.

- Ask your organisation what else it could consider implementing. Apply the Pareto Principle, 20% of your effort contributing to 80% of the result, to these suggestions.

This is a critical step. Think of risk not as an activity but as a capability. Build the capability as it will allow your organisation to scale. Things may not go entirely to plan all the time, but with this capability being constantly practiced, the consequences will be avoided or minimised.

Finally, consider the idea that no action results in a greater future action. *What?* All organisations are dynamic and to remain static is not an option. The rate of action will present a greater degree of risk if:

- The choice is to do the minimum: By so doing, a larger transformation is potentially looming.

- Transformation is underway: Statistically, 80–90% of transformations fail as objectives aren't realised.

Therefore, by building a risk capability within the organisation, there is a greater potential for well-managed iterations to create a shift for the organisation. Iteration sits between minimal action and transformation. By being in a state of iteration, constant sustained shifts can be achieved, which will increase the probability of averting a transformation.

Rightsizing and redundancies

This is a difficult topic to write and talk about openly. It's like discussing politics, sex, and religion among adults. There are lots of private thoughts and limited opportunities for shared understanding (note this is understanding and not agreement).

It's inevitable that your organisation will right-size at some stage, and it's likely that roles will be made redundant and good people impacted. Due to the dynamic nature of the technology industry, technology teams potentially have more frequent cycles of rightsizing. The intended outcomes are often not realised and this results in future remediation (i.e. more rightsizing). Further, people's contributions are eroded due to fear, poor leadership and a lack of career management know-how.

Here you will read about my professional learnings with some personal insights based on decades of experience either watching and learning or leading these initiatives. Most technology executives today need to build new capabilities or integrate shadow capabilities into their organisations. There is often a limited budget to do this, plus an overlapping of capabilities regarding the current technical capability and the desired technical currency. These are two different things that will be explained. Unfortunately, rightsizing organisations for the future will be a necessary skill for any technical executive due to the dynamic nature of the industry.

Let's wind back. I first commenced working in the late 80s, having not completed high school (more on this later). In the first part of my career, I observed two waves of redundancies: one in the early 1990s, another just after 2000 and significant changes after 2008. Observing these periods has offered some key lessons as to why some of these changes went better than others:

- A person is not to be made redundant—a role is; unfortunately, the person is implicated in the role. Organisations that do this well remind everyone of this at the initial planning, during, and at the end of the process. People directly impacted must be reminded that they have not done anything wrong and that *they* are not being dismissed—it's their role that is no longer required.

- The implications within an organisation post-redundancy are varied and the dip in motivation can be longer than desired if people are treated poorly, information is limited or there is no compelling sense of meaningful work to progress. In this regard, fear of further reductions is not the appropriate motivation.

- Ideally undertake this activity once every 24 months. Don't assume you will have the luxury of tweaking here and there over 12 to 18 months. Generally, you need to go deeper than you think—there are opportunities in doing this (more on this later). In addition, the tweaking approach has people walking on eggshells and focusing on survival rather than doing great work. Great work, on occasion, involves debate and disagreement, sometimes with senior leaders, but people are less likely to engage in the debate if they are only focusing on survival. Building an environment/culture of constructive conflict is a key tenant to achieving your digital potential.

- Support for leaders is to be provided beyond HR and beyond the odd text message and email from a colleague saying, *this is the right thing to do, good luck, and I am here if you need me.* Such messages are nice, but they are not supportive. Support comes from talking through scenarios with peers who have had the same experience. Sharing experiences is an opportunity to improve the experience for the employees directly impacted and the broader team. It also grows the confidence for the leader by being less robotic and demonstrating a genuine empathy with everyone.

- Executive assistants (EAs) also need to be supported. A great EA is emotionally invested with the organisation and the people they support. Additionally, they are likely to know, before many others, who will be impacted. Don't assume you know the type of support that suits everyone. Ask your EA.

- Every organisation has slightly different processes and support available. Sometimes, the support that is offered to directly impacted employees is optional and based on executive discretion. Make this support available to employees (such as outplacement). Sometimes, executives choose not to make this available to employees due to the cost involved. However, there is a greater cost in not offering this, potentially delaying the impacted employee from moving through what is next for them (they may talk about this to their colleagues, who endeavour to help but are not qualified to do so, distracting both parties from focusing on what is important) and negatively impacting on the perception of the extent to which people are valued by those remaining.

The above lessons are still relevant. Going further, how can one imagine a better organisation for the future with fewer roles? The 'rule of thirds' has proven to be true in several technology organisations across very different industries. When I have been asked to reduce costs and to consider role reductions, there were three types of contribution these roles made.

Roles generally align to the following three criteria:

- Technically critical: Roles that are technically critical support key technologies; however, avoid ring-fencing multiple roles. The reality is that a lot of technology is now being automated, which presents opportunities to rationalise multiple roles in the same area.
- Leadership critical: This is not about senior leaders, it's about key leadership roles within the organisation. These

roles may not manage people but could offer key thought leadership or capability (e.g. Commercial Manager, Business Analyst, and Risk and Control Manager).

- Additional roles: These are the roles that are involved in the work but are not critical to it. They 'swim with' initiatives rather than being 'key' to them and potentially increase the drag on initiatives through additional conversations that offer limited value. They may be involved due to their legacy technology knowledge rather than current knowledge, and their involvement is habitual rather than critical.

As leaders, you will align people's roles to the three categories. As you embark on this activity, go deeper than you think may be necessary. When analysing the possible roles that are no longer relevant, consider this as an opportunity to improve the capability of the organisation. Removing a third of roles at one time is challenging; however, removing 10–20% of roles and replacing the remaining 10–20% with the right roles is like lightening the load and adding a turbo.

An example is the production of reports within an organisation. You may consider removing the traditional business analyst who compiled the reports and replacing this with a data automation and integration capability. This will automate the manual production, create scale and reduce a point of failure.

The most optimal timing for these changes is augmenting the organisation by hiring for the new roles then shrinking it once these roles are filled by removing those that are no longer required. Completing this within the first half of the financial year generally results in current year savings. If this is not an option, project-based work and items on a team's Agile backlog may need to be paused for a period. Based on my professional experience, other executives across the business are supportive of slowing down for a short period in order to go faster later.

As an employee, here is what you can do to avoid the probability of redundancy:

- Technical currency: Don't become confused with technical capability. Technical currency is what is and will be current for the next period. How can this be incorporated into your role, if it is not already?

- Leadership capability: What is your gift? Find this and cultivate it. Make yourself the person who everybody wants on their project or in their Agile scrum.

- Learning: No one is ever complete. Be on the lookout for learning experiences. I didn't complete high school; however, I went back to night school for my under- and postgraduate studies. Every year, I prioritise some form of professional learning as an extension of my current role. Writing this book has been great learning.

- Organisational knowledge: At one of my previous organisations, there was a person who was developing software on legacy technology; however, as a result, this person also had wonderful operational knowledge. This knowledge became the currency for their future role. They de-invested in the technology capability (it was no longer current) and led the developers of the preferred software solution to create the new application. It was inspiring to watch and a great example to others.

- Treat everybody as you would like to be treated: It feels good to be welcomed by others, and it's even better to be included in many things due to the type of person you are. Make yourself a person who everybody wants to spend time with—being included allows your role to evolve.

This is a difficult topic, but it's something that should be discussed more often within leadership teams and their people. By discussing this more regularly, thoughts will evolve, and actions will be implemented. These actions are likely to reduce the need for radical transformation and enable more frequent transitions through active management; thus, creating a future-oriented relevant organisation.

Managing your career

In 2002, I qualified as a coactive coach. I still regularly practise these skills.

At time of writing this book, at least twice to possibly three times a fortnight, I receive a message from a former colleague or somebody I have met within the industry. Sometimes these people are working at a technology organisation, sometimes they are from overseas and, for clarity, very few of them work for my most recent employer. People seem to reconnect with me from several jobs back; it's as if time creates a boomerang. Generally, they want to ask what I think about something, or they are seeking advice about their career. I don't like giving advice. I don't think I am good at giving advice and when people have tried to give me advice in the past, I found it was their perspective rather than what was most suitable for me.

Further, having met so many people, I don't know *exactly* who they are, what they are great at or why they have chosen to contact me. When you don't know somebody well, it is difficult to give advice. My immediate internal response is *this is interesting.* I wonder why they have chosen to contact me and what can I learn from it? Learning is one of my primary drivers. This curiosity benefits both the person contacting me and myself.

There is one constant though. I am almost always contacted when something has happened or is about to happen. A person may be about to make a decision or they find themselves in a situation beyond their control. Sometimes they are in a dilemma; they are uncertain weighing up opportunities, angry, emotional, confused, frustrated or potentially excited about something. One former, more senior and exceptionally capable individual once referred to me as his priest (I am not deeply religious— this was his term and is not intended to be used in a defamatory manner) as he felt he could share things with me that he couldn't with others.

When I reflect on this, I think *my curiosity and my willingness to learn from others with no judgement* indirectly makes people more comfortable in sharing things with me. Particularly people in organisations who are more senior to me, whether it is my immediate reporting manager or their peer who is wrestling with something. I have known others who have exhibited the *traits above,* and they have had similar experiences. These people seek to support others without anything in return; they have no expectation that anything will be returned from that individual. There is no intention of a future arrangement.

There have been people I have worked with who have endeavoured to cultivate a close relationship with me; however, it has not felt genuine and I have distanced myself either consciously or subconsciously. This was due to a lack of genuineness from that person and where there was an intention behind the interaction. As a result, I was less personally open and vulnerable; they didn't see the best version of me. This is a pity for everyone when it happens. There is no doubt that many of us operate in this manner, almost all the time, for fear of judgement then consequence.

People are generally not prepared to share things. They don't say what they are truly thinking and opportunities that offer diversity of thought remain unrealised. If you can, try doing something without an expectation of anything in return. You may receive a greater gift than what you expected—the gift of learning.

When I am contacted by somebody, I generally start by asking how they are and *not* why are they contacting me or what has happened. Their response then directs me to the next question or statement, but very early on I remind people of what Steve Jobs said at Stanford.

> 'You can't connect the dots looking forward; you can only connect them looking backwards. So, you have to trust that the dots will somehow connect in your future.'
>
> —Steve Jobs

These conversations have created great learnings for me. Some common themes have emerged, and these are being shared in the spirit of what I have *learned*. Here are my learnings so far. I have no doubt that this list will change in this dynamic world (more on this later).

Philosophical learnings

1. A mentor of mine once said that your 20s are for being educated, your 30s are for gaining experience and your 40s are for harvesting. If you strive for one prior to the other, it will erode your potential. It's important you know where you are at, don't rush things as later things will unravel. Further, how do you know when you are capable of harvesting? You can transition to a new industry by bringing your capability.

2. It's unlikely your current employer will remain your lifetime employer. Accept this and be grateful for all

experiences (the great, good and indifferent). *These are the dots that will connect at some stage.*

3. How are you remaining current? Seek to learn something new every year. Share with others what you are learning.

4. Practice being open. I am an Australian living on an island at the bottom of the world. Our family spent nine years living and working on top of the world. This expanded our minds and made us more open to everything. You don't have to move halfway around the world to be open: what could you do to be more open? Being open presents opportunities. How are you expanding your mind?

5. Look inside to be the best version of yourself outside. Don't endeavour to replicate others, learn from them; however, avoid copying. Copying takes a lot of energy and is not genuine; people will know when somebody is not genuine. Your greatest strength is the fact that nobody else is like you. Seek to be the best version of yourself.

6. If something is uncomfortable, determine if there is support with the uncomfortableness. Judgement is not support, don't confuse somebody telling you what to do with how you can explore what you should do.

Much of the above is about mindset. These learnings may be appropriate for you at some stage. Or they may never be appropriate and you may seek insights from elsewhere. Whatever works for you, do it.

The next six learnings are about action. The world has changed dramatically this century and there is a lot of commentary about this. Most data in the world has been created this century, nothing is static, and we now live in a dynamic data world. Consider this as context regarding the suggested actions below.

The information on your LinkedIn profile, other jobsite profiles and contained within your resume is static. Our world is a dynamic content creating one and you need to consider if you will participate in this, and if so, how?

Practical suggestions

1. Do you have a domain (a www address)? It could be your name, it could be a company or community you are wanting to create or be part of. Consider creating this community. I own both www.changelead.com and www. davidbanger.com, plus some other similar domains. One is my current business platform and the other is now the website where you can find out more about me and this book. When I first registered those domains, I didn't know their purpose; however, I found that if I continue to discover when the time is right, the ideas will emerge.

2. What are the five to ten things you know? Start writing or shooting a video about them. Create the content on your domain/website first, then share it on other platforms. These platforms will help you find your community. Connect and serve that community without an expectation. If you are passionate about what you have learned, others within your community will be interested. Make sure you have a home for your content; at some stage, you may want to bring it all together, so begin with the end in mind.

3. Accept that you may not be in paid employment. This may or may not be your choice. Be prepared for this and consider what you will do in this instance. The steps directly above this point are important. It's best to start thinking about these things when you are employed. There is some anxiety in putting yourself 'out there';

however, imagine living a life without sharing your thoughts and potential with the world.

4. Be passionate about something. Be restless until you find this. For me it's business first, then people and then technology. What is your order and why are these things important? Share this sooner rather than later. When I started blogging publicly, I was surprised by who and how people read me. I learned how best to channel my areas of interest to an audience. Learn from others while you are sharing. Don't leave yourself wondering what you could be sharing.

5. Know your value and be prepared for everybody not to value it. What? Yes, not everybody will 'get you'; however, don't lose your voice. You may be pleasantly surprised by who will value you and what they will give back.

6. Often, I am asked about the one sure thing to do. After reading the above, what do you think you should do? It could be reading that book you have not yet read or revisiting a YouTube video or TED talk (*as you may have already gathered, Steve Jobs' Stanford Commencement Speech* is my favourite), taking a long walk to order your thoughts or setting aside time to further reflect on the question.

The world is dynamic and will continue to evolve. By applying the approaches of yesterday, you may not realise your potential for tomorrow. The thoughts here are intended to help you think and then act.

Employee experience creates an advantage

If your employees are dynamic, your organisation is potentially at risk of losing them. Jacob Morgan is the author of *The Employee Experience Advantage* (2017). This book offers insight into how an organisation can become more relevant with its employees. Jacob's book was possibly inspired by his question to many C-level executives: 'If your culture was a pill, would you take it?' Almost all answered no.

His early research established that companies that potentially have a 'take-able' pill appoint managers who truly want others to be more successful than they are. Further, these organisations have a co-ordinated one-team approach to:

- Culture
- Technology
- Space

This approach creates an Employee Experience Advantage (EEA). Jacob furthered this research with a team of data scientists who reviewed companies on published 'best' lists. Some organisations appeared on these lists at least and up to forty times. They all embodied an EEA, in addition to benefiting from:

- Being three times more profitable.
- Having 40% less turnover.
- Having 24% less employees to revenue when compared to similar organisations.

These organisations focused on some consistent themes across their vision, mission and values:

- They had a genuine reason of being. This rallied employees to consider their impact on their role and within the broader community.

- People in 'positions of power' cared about others: 'people' were appointed to senior roles with little or no emphasis on technical competency.

- All organisations knew their people well through the use of <u>appropriate</u> data tracking, people-related metrics and genuine dialogue.

- They think like a lab and less like a factory.

These are important points for leadership. Often, when leaders are initially appointed, they are tempted to focus on their subject matter expertise and managing the details.

As a new leader, be mindful of reverting to what you are comfortable with. If you are becoming directly involved in doing the work of your team, your capacity to lead the team is reduced. Also, the example being set may result in your leadership team doing the work of its immediate team. This could result in losing empowerment and the capacity to deal with escalations due to being stretched by working in the technology and not on it. Additionally, growth opportunities within the team may be limited as the leaders are doing some of the work. Limiting these learnings will, in turn, limit how much the team could scale across more meaningful work in the future.

Becoming relevant as a first-time executive

When I was appointed to my first senior technology leadership role, I had three long conversations with people who were far more senior and experienced than myself. I did a lot of listening and asked the odd question; it was a little daunting. They acknowledged that I could manage the team; however, the role was more than this. There was an expectation that I could make a great contribution to the broader business.

After reflecting upon the conversations, I concluded three things. The beauty of this organisation was the culture of empowerment, but this came with significant expectations. It was up to me to either make or lose it—the organisation was unbreakable.

After twelve months being in the role, I asked those leaders if the conclusions were right. They turned the question on me! I replied, 'well if this is working for you, it's working for the team, and I am loving it.'

What made you relevant in the past is unlikely to make you relevant in the future. Here are three areas that you may need to evolve based on my experiences.

Leading the team

- Connect the group and have them co-create how they would like to work with one another.

- Establish a shared space. On the walls, make visible what you are working on, and make sure these things are measured.

- Hire people who are smarter and different to you and encourage them to have a voice. Your role is to work with the business. Seek to create broader connections within the industry to anticipate what is next and avoid the temptation of working in the technology team.

- Lead by sharing your 'values'. Don't replace your organisation's values but define what each one means to you. If a decision is required and the 'values' are in place, the team generally makes the right one.

Influencing the broader business

- Involve others in the emergence of the team, explain what the team is and what it will be doing, and set out the stall. For technology leaders, this is likely to include a strategic document for three years (1000 days) and a quarterly business plan (every 100 days), refreshed and reissued quarterly.

- Prioritisie the business first, then the people and then technology. Technology should support a process or resolve a problem rather than be implemented because it's interesting. Acknowledge that businesses, geographies and departments mature at different rates and align what is next for them, not what is best.

- Get out into the business and build genuine relationships with those in the organisation. Seek to serve your colleagues but not be subservient and be prepared to constructively challenge.

Involving others in your thinking is as simple as sharing it. At two different organisations, I led teams who created an annual video of 'a day in the life of the employee at the organisation'. I can recall at least half a dozen videos being created over the years. As well as communicating the business plan, we created videos to show how using the technology would benefit the technology team's initiatives.

'For a time I didn't want to answer any questions about Queen. I'd like to be viewed as something alive and relevant, not some fossil.'

—Brian May

Many people don't read detailed plans, but they will watch a video. Beyond these being a great way to communicate, they are also very effective in building the technology team's culture. The videos started with an alarm in the morning, a series of personal and professional events and activities during the day and concluded at home. Creating these does not have to be expensive; within your organisation you will find many talents. At one of my organisations, we had an employee who captured videos on the weekends as a wedding photographer. This person was very happy to shoot the video and required less of a brief than an external agency. Our costs were minimal, just the hiring of some equipment and the purchase of a new PC so footage could be edited. These videos were also useful for international audiences and on several occasions, we were able to add the language of our visitors within the video.

Sharing thinking

- Some teams serve multiple functions, connect one function with another and encourage idea sharing. These are not your ideas. Sometimes, you may mature an idea so it can scale; however, it is far more effective to be a facilitator of an idea rather than owning it.

- Sharing something weekly, at the same time, in the same way. At a previous organisation, I was responsible for measuring culture. I learnt something interesting about some of the well-regarded leaders. They communicated weekly in their words, their notes included an industry perspective, something their team was working on and something small about themselves. When I started to do this, it helped me connect with my team and others across the organisation.

- Being available to listen. Many, upon finding their voice, want to shout and be the most dominant voice in any room all the time. The gift of finding your voice is to allow others to share their voice. If you establish a platform, share the stage with others. Remember, this is about sharing everyone's thinking, not just yours.

A big learning for anyone transitioning into a leadership role is dependency on 'others' for outcomes. Micromanagement is not sustainable, good people will leave and you will become exhausted. The 'others' are beyond your immediate leadership team; they are potentially across the organisation and external to your organisation. Sometimes first-time leaders adopt a combative approach with those external organisations that serve them. Initially this may have some cost benefit; however, over time value is almost always diminished. These others could potentially be a key contributor to how your organisation can innovate.

> 'Motivation comes from working on things we care about. It also comes from working with people we care about.'
> —Sheryl Sandberg

Additionally, they could be a source of greater relevance, leading to connection with customers and broader communities.

Guy Kawasaki's inspiration for greater relevance

Guy Kawasaki has learned from those who have participated and contributed to shifts. He is very apt at putting things in context and worked at Apple twice in his career. Guy is forthright with his views and offers sharp insights.

> 'I am now two-thirds dead; why should I
> be concerned about what people think.'
>
> —Guy Kawasaki

Here is what I have learned from attending several of Guy's keynotes. These four points resonated with the relevance section and Guy has many additional points that are well worth considering.

Make meaning rather than money

When clarifying your meaning, it should achieve at least one of these three factors:

- Increase the quality of life.

- Right a wrong.

- Prevent the end of something good.

When considering a change, avoid acting until you find meaning. Then, check to see if at least one of the three above factors is the meaning behind the action.

Start from the bottom

Avoid falling into the common trap of segmenting populations, calculating future revenue of only a % of the population and converting this to profit. Consider how you weave your 'MAT':

- **M**ilestones. For example, the design or shipping of a product is a milestone; whereas, setting up an office is not. Avoid being distracted by the mundane. Basically, milestones are something you would tell everyone about.

- **A**ssumptions need to be made. Consider sales efforts (calls and meetings), ROI, installation costs and anything else that contributes to the achievement of milestones.

- **T**asks are different to assumptions. What activities are undertaken for the assumptions to meet the milestones?

Become a storyteller regarding how you started, what you are doing and where you are going.

Don't be perfect and iterate

Not everything has to be perfect; if you don't cringe when you look back at the first version of something, then it hasn't been shaped fast enough.

Be prepared to iterate quickly—version 1.1, 1.2 or 2.0.

Value and uniqueness

Consider two matrices: value and uniqueness. There's no point being unique without value, as nobody will be interested. Having value without uniqueness equals competition and reduces margins.

When value and uniqueness intersect, businesses endure, and margins can be maintained and increased.

When listening to Guy, it is evident that he has been influenced by his Apple experiences and is a great storyteller. Steve Jobs was also a great storyteller; he had the ability to simplify the complicated and anticipate what people potentially didn't know they needed. He created relevance. I have visited and worked with many people from Apple over many years and something that their people have regularly shared is the ability of their colleagues to tell a story.

How? No more than 10 slides for 20 mins with 30pt font. Somebody at Apple told me that Steve Jobs only used 200pt font.

This approach works. Having spoken at many industry events and as an adjunct professor, my lectures have always consisted of pictures or data and not detailed text. People will listen rather than read, it creates a greater connection. This principle inspired 'the pictures' I created for this book. If you are being asked to present on topic, avoid the temptation trap of listing bullet points and looking and talking to these. Use visuals instead and structure the conversation.

I am a big fan of acronyms and the concept of threes and fives— this book is an example. When speaking about the D-I-R-T-Y model, I immediately have five sections and will require areas under each section. This is twenty pieces of content:

- Each letter of the D-I-R-T-Y acronym (5 sections)
- Three points under each section (15 sections)

Further, subject to the brief, you can either choose to cover all sections or go deeper into a section. The beauty of this approach is you can use images and tell stories that make your content more personable, memorable and relevant.

Start thinking about your stories. Document them and simplify them so they are relatable.

Relevance recap

The Relevance section is broad; here is a succinct snapshot:

- **Risk:** build the **capability across employees** as it will increase the velocity of delivery.

- Rightsizing: avoid tinkering and **analyse roles by their technical and leadership criticality**. The remaining additional roles are areas of opportunity.

- Proactively **manage your career**, determine how you will **dynamically interact** and **serve the broader community**.

- Employee **experience creates an advantage** for organisations. **Be more like a lab** and less like a factory.

- As a **first-time** technology **executive,** focus on **leading your team, influencing** the broader **business,** and **sharing thinking**.

- When **presenting, use pictures** with less or *no* words.

PART 4

INNOVATION

Lots of talk; however, what works?

At some stage, everyone in every organisation has heard that they need to be more innovative. Processes are set up (i.e. innovation application), time is set within the day (i.e. innovation meetings), bodies are formed (i.e. an innovation steering group) and a traditional, organisational-structured mentality is applied to something that is probably best left in a state of flow as opposed to being orchestrated.

How best can innovation be defined?

Fifteen experts were asked, and an ultimate definition was 'executing an idea which addresses a specific challenge and achieves value for both the company and customer'. (Skillicorn, 2019)

There is innovation fatigue within many organisations, which results from being an addition to something rather than a part of something. How can an organisation go from a dedicated time or team to having innovation as part of people's work and creating a state of 'innovation flow'?

> 'Flow with whatever may happen and let your mind be free. Stay centred by accepting whatever you are doing. This is the ultimate.'
> —Zhuangzi

Flow means being in the zone, being fully immersed, highly energised, and enjoying the process.

Organisations and their employees need to consider being in a constant state of flow, where innovation is part of the flow rather than the sole purpose of the flow. Balance is important within teams. The flow should incorporate many factors from all team members and enable the organisation to realise its potential and mitigate vulnerabilities.

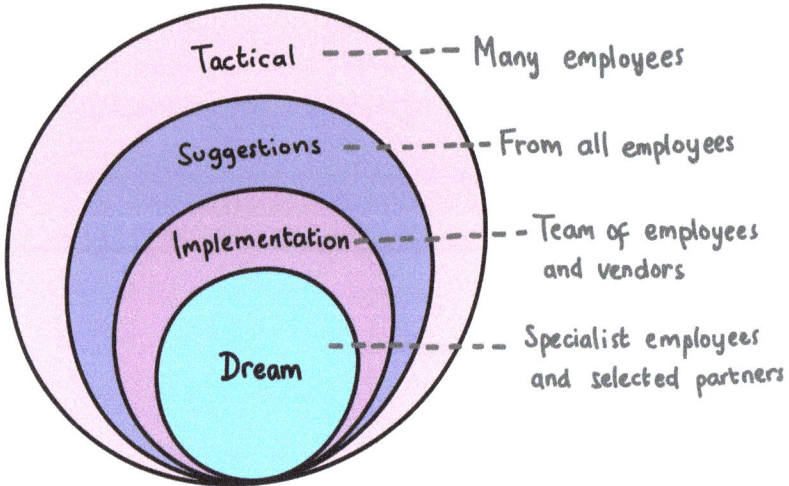

Figure 6: Enterprise innovation ecosystem

There are four spectrums that contribute to an organisation's innovation potential:

- Setting the right conditions: what is most suitable for your organisation?

- Consider areas of tactical focus.

- Encourage employees to suggest ideas then select and implement the most relevant.

- What is your dream and how can this be broken into parts?

Be mindful of both fads and partners, they have their place; however, avoid being overly led or dependent on them. Select partners based on unique capabilities that complement your dreams.

> 'Small groups of people can have
> a really huge impact.'
>
> —Larry Page

Avoid asking for innovation. Set conditions that enable 'it'. Be clear with employees on how they can best contribute to 'it' and try not to talk about 'it'.

Experiences and history that set the right conditions

Many organisations continue to wrestle with how they innovate, but there are learnings from the past that we can apply now and into the future.

Encourage diversity of thought

The story of Ada Lovelace[3] was included on a portable poster on a corridor outside an executive meeting room and breakout area. Many people walked past this poster at the organisation I was employed at, but not many—if any—stopped. One day I moved the poster into the breakout area whilst meeting some graduates.

Ada—daughter of the great English poet Byron—was, in the early 1800s, the first person to document a computer software program as an algorithm. (Wow! Just wow!) For Ada, learning was exceptionally important. She was tutored by Charles Babbage, who was paid by the British Government to explore technical hardware. Ada was inspired. She explored what could be achieved with the hardware and developed 'software' language. Ada's mother sought to balance her creative side— passed on from her father—with some mathematics, which was Babbage's role.

Byron spoke of the risks of change and actively resisted change. Byron was a Luddite; whereas, Ada challenged this and encouraged diversity of thought. I reminded the graduates of Ada's story and explained how their fresh perspectives could challenge our existing thoughts. There was an immediate connection with the graduates, and I asked them to hold me accountable if they ever thought I was a Luddite. This is an effective way of looking at events of the past that can influence people's involvement in creating the future.

Welcome ideas from people who are capable and comfortable with being themselves. Identify and embrace those who are a little different and potentially controversial.

Technology reduces costs and enhances capability

Every end of life technology presents an opportunity to move to the next generation of technology. On many occasions I have found that the next generation of technology offers more at a reduced cost for the organisation.

'I sold my most valuable possession, but I knew because I worked at Hewlett Packard, I could buy the next model calculator the very next month for a lower price than I sold the older one for!'

—Steve Wozniak

We carry more technology in our pockets than what put man on the Moon. Technology through innovation improves capability at reduced cost. The first prototype chip for the Apollo guidance computer cost $1,000, and by the time it was in regular use, it cost $25. This innovation greatly assisted in the development of the microchip used in devices for ordinary consumers.[4]

Sensible timing and a structured approach can reduce costs and create possibilities; this helps business cases.

What are your upcoming investments? What is coming to the end of its life? What opportunities could be possible?

For a prototype, what technology costs are exorbitant? Could they be dramatically reduced by the time the service or product is ready for market?

Consider not only timing to market but timing of the capability that will be ready for market.

Strive for greater diversity with flexibility

Many of my employers offered flexible working because they considered it a benefit. Some of my most productive days were outside the workplace and outside of core hours. This is an 'enabler' rather than a 'retainer' of employees. Many industries are approaching this in different ways yet too many still think of this as a retainer. Unfortunately, on many occasions, I have witnessed comments made by others to create guilt. We must be better than this.

> ## 'Too many rules stifle innovation.'
> —Sergey Brin

Bill Hewlett and Dave Packard managed three shifts of workers (many with women) through flexible working patterns in the 1970s. In this sense, the key role of women contributed greatly to the technology industry. The workers were given plenty of leeway for determining how to accomplish objectives and for applying diversity of thought; and management hierarchies were flattened when merged with this flexible approach. Thus, diversity of thought with flexibility will contribute to great outcomes.[5]

How truly liberal is your organisation (beyond a flexible working policy)? What policies are in place? What unwritten policies are holding people back? Why do the people who are a little different leave? What needs to change? Are you pioneering anything for your people? What will encourage their further efforts?

What is a symbol that would signal this?

There are multiple generations within the workforce that represent a great opportunity to generate a diverse range of thought; however, are we too focused on the generation that is entering the workforce?

Should your organisation be more focused on those countries that have left poverty and, in a global world, are entering our markets? Scarcity creates creativity.

Do we need to incorporate more balance or even shift thinking from generational to emerging global?

How is your organisation bringing about diverse global thought?

Casual connections spark ideas

A former employer had an executive bathroom in a building where we all worked. The interesting aspect about the bathroom was not the limited access but what it represented. It was all rather formal and respectful. Only a few years later, another employer had a much more liberal campus including a well-known coffee chain and sofas. As you would expect, there was a stark difference in how employees interacted within these organisations.

I made connections in many organisations; I wanted to build the bridges I would cross in the future. One of these was on a tow path next to a canal and the train station we used to commute to another office. People regularly walked along the tow path as it was time allocated within their diary for travel. I used this allocated time to connect with people on the path. Another employer had a bus station to take employees to another location. While waiting for the bus casual connections were made.

A lot of thought and money goes into creating spaces. I have worked with some truly awesome people who do this amazingly well; it's the little things that can make a difference and they strive to do that. I visited a technology company campus in North America that focused on paths and long grass. People had to take the path to avoid walking through the long grass. Again, while people were on the move they connected.

Strive to make spaces that create casual connections and allow people to converse.

Also I am a strong advocate for 'walking meetings'. The moving body helps the mind and taking those who may not be as senior as you, within an organisation, out for a walk can loosen things up.

However, this all started long before this century. Robert Noyce,[6] nicknamed the *Mayor of Silicon Valley,* and an MIT graduate, developed a more open and unstructured workplace after working in a rigid hierarchy. He was a key initiator of the 'Californian lifestyle of work', and his objective was to enable ideas to be sparked, dissented to, refined, and applied without 'people having to go up through a chain of command'. The *Mayor* created a true meritocracy by empowering employees, which resulted in them being more entrepreneurial.

How often has an idea been initiated within your organisation and something prototyped?

How can an employee or group within your organisation initiate a prototype? Who has prototyped something and how was this supported and shared?

Are you building energy in this area or exasperating people?

What is being learned by the leadership and employees as these items are introduced? How are people being conditioned? Conditioning will influence future efforts.

What could be prototyped and how could this be accelerated?

How many meetings could be walking meetings? Schedule something now.

Ideas must be combined with business skills

Sometimes the technology team will endeavour to innovate in isolation and 'surprise' the business with something great. This is often unsuccessful due to a lack of connection and because the innovation is sometimes based on a theory rather than real world occurrences of the organisation. It frustrates those in the broader organisation and creates trust issues. Remember Part 2: Technology?

Several organisations I have worked with or offered services to have created a STIG: sounds cool, right? But what is it? *System and Technology Improvement/Initiative/Innovation* (take your pick) *Group.* One organisation considered Governance for the 'G'. It was a fleeting thought and was not implemented. People will interpret the intent of something often through the label. Sometimes you may wish to consider involving people in establishing the STIG or equivalents because they will own it and want to champion it. The STIG has representatives from many areas of the organisation and considers many scenarios.

> 'Intuition is nothing but the outcome
> of earlier intellectual experience.'
> —Albert Einstein

Ideas should be shared with diverse audiences so they can be evolved. Such audiences will include deep technologists and those who are savvy with business.

Further, the culture of an organisation needs to be supportive of how to enable innovation. For example, there are ideas from the 'hippie movement' that helped define Silicon Valley (Isaacson, 2015):

- Authority should be questioned.
- Hierarchies should be circumvented.
- Non-conformity should be admired.
- Creativity should be nurtured.

As cross-functional teams collaborate more frequently and intensely, skills are being transferred and technologists are building business skills (and vice versa). This should be encouraged; study where it is working well in your organisation and replicate it.

What ideas are stuck?

When an idea becomes stuck, how can balance be brought to either exhaust or progress the idea?

Be rational but decisive

There is a temptation for innovation to be something **big** in an organisation; this is potentially influenced by wanting to disrupt. However, for many it will be about building confidence by executing the ideas being presented by those within the organisation. It's important to build momentum and communicate regularly to those offering the ideas as this will aid maintaining the flow of ideas. Not all ideas will be executed immediately and your organisation needs to decide what will be and why.

'Successful innovation leaders cannot allow strategic conversations to stop at the aspirational level. They must insist on drilling down to the next level of managerial choices that are necessary to gain the desired outcome.'

—Bill Fischer

At one organisation, I worked with a team to sort ideas into three initial categories:

- Do now
- Concrete suggestion
- Dreams

Within these categories, there is additional criteria such as alignment to the strategy or if you are considering your digital strategy, what ideas will enable greater customer intimacy or assist with scale? (More on Digital in Part 5.) All ideas should be analysed and feedback should be provided. Ensure feedback is crisp, clean and fair. Some ideas may need to be prototyped and some may need clarification. Encourage this and involve the broader communities—members of the STIG could be very helpful at this stage.

Learn through prototyping and share these learnings across the organisation.

The learnings will create rigour regarding how ideas are matured and improve both the quality of thinking on the ideas of employees and how your organisation assesses them.

Simply smart

The greatest creativity has come from those who have connected the arts and sciences. For example, people like Steve Jobs believed that beauty mattered. True geniuses such as Kepler, Newton, Einstein and Jobs had an instinct for simplicity. Many of us are smart, but can we be simple? Simplicity potentially allows you to reach the largest audience. (Isaacson, 2015)

There was a situation at one of my former employers that required the replacement of a successful legacy technology, which contained up to 200 mini applications that would support various client-based activities. The task was daunting and many had endeavoured to replace the solution. One of my colleagues referred to the exercise as climbing Everest: there were bodies scattered on route from all previous attempts. I proposed something different to the team. We analysed the most common activity completed by the legacy application and made it paperless by moving the activity to a mobile device. The process wasn't complicated; however, the integration of several solutions (for example, a camera on a device or a browser-based application and input of information either via a keyboard or voice) potentially presented issues. The initial experience was the greatest barrier to an ongoing adoption of an alternative solution.

The team piloted a prototype solution with a selected group of employees. They travelled to where the activity was taking place and shadowed those completing it. Some of the employees involved in this process were strong advocates of the legacy technology. The team heard them out and evolved the solution.

When those advocating the legacy solution saw their ideas in the pilot solution, they began contemplating trialling it. This was the turning point; they realised an alternative was possible. My team's motivation went up a gear as it had a genuine modern alternative. It achieved this with a common simple process and by making it paperless. When others, in different locations, heard of the solution, they began asking for it. The broader organisation then shifted its preference from the legacy technology to the replacement technology and a swell was created. This was only possible through addressing a simple task and showing people that by incorporating their ideas they could evolve the solution together.

Prototype the simple and most common first rather than the most promising; it's highly probable that this will have the greatest potential of acceptance in the broader community.

Simplicity is the greatest form of cleverness. Share this as an objective across your organisation.

Divergence delays potential

There are many ideas within organisations and sometimes they are not evolved due to a lack of connection between colleagues. At several of my former employers, I asked various executives to sponsor key objectives of the technology strategy. These strategies generally had between four to six objectives and were referred to as 'themes'. When some executives were asked, laughter often followed and the odd comment about what do I know about technology? My reply: 'what a great opportunity to learn'. They soon developed a greater appreciation of emerging capabilities. Additionally, there was an understanding of the tension between these emerging capabilities with the expectations of an organisation driving demand on tactical initiatives and limited availability of technical resources that could be applied either to one or the other but not both.

Part of their executive sponsorship role was visiting technology organisations that offered Executive Briefing sessions. At one session, a technology was demonstrated in a business scenario. This immediately changed an executive's perception of a certain 'personal' technology. There was a decision pending at another location regarding this technology. This decision had been pending for some time. A visit was scheduled to that location by this executive in the coming months to see a demonstration of how this technology could be used. At this EBC, the executive leaned over to me and said, 'approve that request'.

The technology was then rolled out to other locations and integrated into other initiatives; this would not have been possible without that approval.

Here is a great historical example. The internet and the PC were both born in the 1970s, but they grew separately from one another. There was a difference in mindset between 'networkers' and those 'excited by the PC'. Tim Berners Lee, inventor of the World Wide Web, who tinkered with various technologies that were not as successful as the www, stated: 'We didn't have the same ripe community and cultural mix around us like Homebrew and Silicon Valley'. New ideas occur when random notions are mixed together until they coalesce. As Tim explains, 'They may not fit well, and then we go for a bike ride or something, and it's better'. Exercise the mind as well as the body (Isaacson, 2015). Remember those walking meetings I mentioned earlier?

Beyond mixing the work with another external activity, how are people, teams and departments integrating across the organisation? How could they be more integrated?

Consider establishing platforms (virtual formal teams) that incorporate people from across the organisation based on the type of initiative rather than having the team responsible for managing the service creating it.

Further, make these platforms people's primary team.

Connect your experts

Deciding to leave the corporate world and the support of a large organisation can be daunting. Working by yourself requires discipline to start and finish something; however, excitement can replace discipline with the quality of free information available to help you. YouTube has become *my* colleague. It gives me access to experts everywhere, and I am not bound by corporate policy to determine whether I should do something or not. If it's easy and aligns to the direction of the company, I will do it. My discipline now is not to become distracted and to remind myself to continue to focus on learning rather than entertainment. The potential of video (beyond video conferencing) for information sharing within an organisation is enormous and probably something that will be realised in the future. Those organisations blocking their employees from viewing YouTube should reconsider and instead monitor YouTube activity. Approach this with the spirit of empowering employees with the capability to educate themselves. This is not new; the internet was founded on information sharing.

In June 1993, there were only 130 websites. By June 1995, there were 23,500 and a year later, 257,601.[7] In December 1997, John Barger produced a fun website called *The First Blog*.[8] By Feb 2011, there were 156 million public blogs.[9]

I am now part of several virtual communities. I am connected to experts who have helped me be a better, more effective expert. Operating within the boundaries of your organisation will limit it. Consider *Encyclopaedia Britannica*, which ceased publishing print editions in 2011. In the 1980s, Microsoft approached

Britannica to collaborate on a CD-ROM version but the offer was declined and Britannica continued with its, then, profitable print editions for a period.[10] Wikipedia, launched in 2001, is now the world's online encyclopaedia. With Wikipedia, people were initially concerned about the lack of experts; however, the crowd became the experts—sharing, critiquing and correcting knowledge.

This was achieved in the way that most digital tools get commandeered for social purposes and evolve into communities. Connected communities can disrupt industries.

Who are your experts and how connected are they?

Consider including those experts from the broader community.

Structure creative collaboration

Based on my experience, innovation is unlikely to be successful when undertaken in isolation. It is best when the idea is iterated by a community. That community will require a range of capabilities:

- Those who know the problem or have an idea.
- Those capable of creating the solution.
- Those who know how the solution can be implemented within the organisation.

The experience shared earlier in the *Simply Smart* section had this team emerge as communities were connected to address the situation. When these communities are connected with a greater sense of making meaningful outcomes the difficult becomes possible.

'Steve Jobs didn't really set the direction of my Apple I and Apple II designs, but he did the more important part of turning them into a product that changed the world.'

—Steve Wozniak

Creativity is a collaborative process. Innovation is achieved incrementally, generally through a diverse range of teams working together and not via light-bulb moments: this is why STIGs work. Walter Isaacson's book, *The Innovators*, concludes that innovation requires at least three things:

- A great idea.

- The engineering talent to execute it.

- Business savvy and the deal-making capability to turn it into a successful product.

The best innovators are communities who can link beauty to engineering, humanity to technology and poetry to processes. Visionaries must be partnered with those who can execute; a vision without execution is a mere hallucination.

Many organisations will not be able to implement all the items in italics listed in this section; they may already have some of them implemented and may plan to implement additional areas.

Prior to this, consider:

- *Balancing the areas to ensure there are different types of areas in order to maximise the possibilities.*

- *Building or breaking existing organisational moulds: What will be a moment or a combination of moments that create the right conditions for innovation?*

- *Iterating: The organisations will not get everything right every time. Organisations will need to accept learnings and evolve.*

This activity relates to setting the right conditions for the execution of an idea, linking experiences with historical innovation to emphasise the learning and enabling others to set the conditions for innovation.

There are a range of tactics that can be deployed with this.

A tactical approach to innovation

Is it dedicated time or a dedicated team that aids innovation? Probably neither. As organisations have become aware of the need to evolve more frequently, a range of practices have been adopted and teams implemented, some examples of which include:

- An innovation team dedicated to supporting others in order to help them innovate.

- An innovation suggestion application as an evolution of the traditional suggestion box.

- An innovation steering committee to ensure some guardrails and governance of what, when and how an organisation can innovate ... ohhh.

- Providing people with time for innovation i.e. allocating a percentage of the week to this activity.

- Have Innovation Directors or Chief Innovation Officers in place. Organisations that have introduced these roles have, in many instances, had the role sit on the side of the core functions within organisations with limited influence.

- Innovation meetings. These are for a selected group of people within the organisation, but they can sometimes become clubby so that broader traction and integration are often not realised.

All the above suggestions include the term 'innovation'. Innovation is an *addition* to something rather than a *part* of something. It's being in a state of 'innovation flow'.

Flow means being in the zone, being fully immersed, highly energised, and enjoying the process. Organisations and their employees today should consider being in a constant state of flow, with innovation as part of the flow rather than the sole purpose of the flow.

Flow is not about being frantic. Sporting people explain the flow experience as everything being in slow motion and having the opportunity to see and think about everything. It's not in addition to or separate from something—it is the something. People and teams who have achieved something different were obsessed with resolving a problem. In this regard, their work shifted from activity to problem resolution, and this shift, in perspective, created a greater level of awareness or thought so they could see and think about more.

> 'You can't use up creativity. The more
> you use, the more you have.'
> —Maya Angelou

How can you frame a problem? It's not something the leadership team can create but is something that should come from within a team. Rather than dictating an activity, choice creates a sense of energy, and people will own the activity.

'Problem hunting' is the direction provided by leaders, who should consider hunting in the following areas:

1. Simplify tasks

Be obsessed with this: work that cannot be eliminated should be explored for automation opportunities. As per my earlier example, consider those high volume, non-complex tasks then challenge the existing thinking, and consider if a portion of the future solution could be automated.

What things could be automated?

While analysing high-volume tasks, and if full automation is not an option, what automation could be used for part of a task? Consider the potential of sub-automation.

2. Processes

These are often overlooked and localised by teams. Localisation creates complexity, and this complexity is often due to organisational customs rather than criticality. It's difficult to create scale and consistency when processes are heavily customised due to local customs.

An example of this is pre-start meetings on a project site within the construction industry. All these meetings have a similar objective, which is to discuss the work for the day ahead and keep people safe and the work on schedule. The process for these meetings is heavily localised based on a range of factors including the subjects and the leader. Construction organisations have hundreds of these meetings that occur at the beginning of every shift. Everyone knows the purpose of the meetings, but they are all slightly different. Some organisations have standardised these meetings by working with highly effective project leaders and technology, taking their best practice and making it standard practice.

Consider customer processes. Remember Six Sigma, SIPOCs and COPISs mentioned earlier. Uber emerged as a result of frustrations regarding access to taxis. The customer process was simplified and digitised. Uber invested in two areas: customer experience and scaling. As a result, it created an alternative to the taxi industry by not requiring vehicles—rather, the vehicles join the service. This process was so simple that it was globalised and rapidly adopted by consumers. This consumer adoption occurred because the experience was consistent wherever they travelled, and the customer no longer had to participate/tolerate local taxis with local 'custom processes'.

Digitising internal processes helps an organisation; however, they should not be the defaulted digital strategy. The activity can build capability and confidence to tackle bigger things but those bigger things need to be business related (more on this in Part 5).

3. Intelligent data

Organisations capture, manage, and refine data. Very simply, there are two types of data: useful and non-useful. The data may or may not be big and may or may not be within a data lake, and sometimes both things confuse the intended outcome of the data. Often, useful data has been identified by organisations but is polluted by non-useful data that is creating distractions or potential distortions as a result of a big data agenda or other fad agendas. (One of my teams spent several months on a fad agenda with a global vendor—be careful of vendors' data agendas.)

Data that is useful can offer insights into something. At a previous organisation, my team analysed data from a range of different locations within which there was a connection made to a certain activity that was not commercial in nature but was being consistently applied. Through this consistent discipline of a particular action, it was evident that other actions were being undertaken with the same discipline and there was a greater probability of the stated commercial outcomes. As a result of this intelligence, the organisation was able to forecast areas of commercial challenge in advance due to a certain activity not occurring. This data was neither big nor in a data lake, it was an insight.

Seek to develop an intelligence capability beyond the practice of data management. Rather than considering the amount of data under management, consider instead the intelligence gleaned from the data.

4. Digital basics

The terms 'data' and 'digital' are sometimes used interchangeably by non-technical executives because there is an expectation that data is digital—it is not. Data may help digital, but it is not digital.

Digital is the merging of the physical and digital worlds of space and place. Simplification, process standardisation and intelligent data may identify an opportunity for taking a physical activity into a digital realm. Teams I have worked with in the past have set an objective to 'delight' the broader organisation with something that wasn't expected. Another team called this activity 'truffle hunting'. Both activities were based on a couple of objectives.

'Delight' and 'truffles' in a digital context should remove barriers that either create distance with end customers or keep you bound to a supplier or partner model that erodes the potential of a digital ecosystem. Set these as the priorities and consider what other savvy innovation approaches could assist in achieving the outcomes.

5. Partners

There is a considerable amount of investment within many global technology companies. Start with areas that intersect or overlap with existing services or products being offered.

Avoid reinventing this, as your organisation is unlikely to have their R&D budgets.

An emerging example would be 'Internet of Things' capabilities developed by a technology company that could be leveraged by an engineering business that integrates smart sensor technologies into construction in order to improve maintenance practices by means of the early detection of changes.

In order to enable a digital business model, consider how your technology partners can help with the automation, scale and intelligence relevant to your industry.

6. People

Reduce the isolation of employees and partners and seek to integrate people across the organisation who may have different reporting lines by setting a common objective based on a shared area of work. These teams may benefit from some modern working practices but be careful with your expectations of these practices and seek vertical alignment within the team.

When an objective becomes the overwhelming sense of a team's collective purpose rather than their reporting line, different things may happen.

Finally, the six points above are not technologies. Technology contributes to achieving an outcome and exists within certain philosophies, but it should not be the purpose of daring to be different. Furthermore, the technology team should not be the sole source of these activities. The technology team will and should be involved, but a collective group of people across an organisation offers far greater potential.

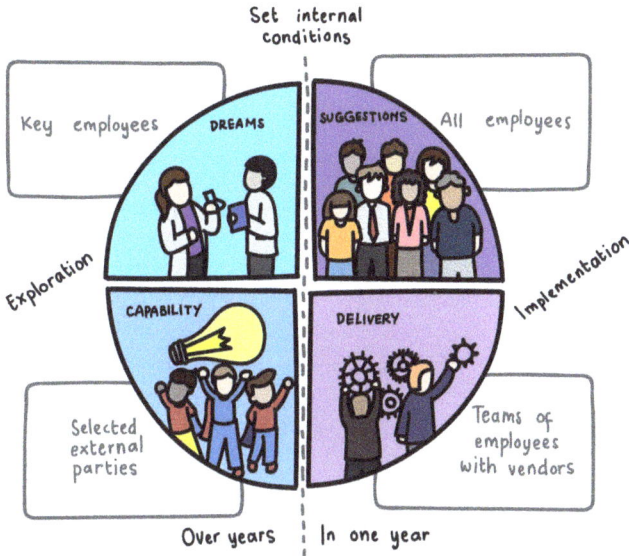

Figure 7: Enterprise innovation players

Dreaming and strategic technical innovation

Sometimes an organisation will decide to take a longer view on what and how they intend to innovate. This happened at Tesla where the goal was the same at the time of writing the book as it was a decade ago: 'to accelerate the advent of sustainable transport by bringing compelling mass market electric cars to market as soon as possible'.[11] Tesla has now released three models and at the Tesla Model 3 launch, Elon Musk explained how each have served an innovation purpose:

- The Tesla Roadster: high price and low volume. It showed the world you could make an electronic car.

- The Tesla Model S: lower price and mid volume. Taking the learnings from the Roadster and applying these to an everyday sedan electric car. The market and customers liked SUVs as much as sedans, so the Tesla Model X was introduced to meet those expectations. The revenue from both vehicles helped the next stage of innovation.

- The Tesla Model 3: affordable price and high volume. This was possible due to the earlier stages of the innovation process.

Strategic technical innovation will require investment prior to mass market penetration. The identification and agreement of milestones for this innovation approach are important as the return on the investment could potentially be delayed.

> 'Software innovation, like almost every other kind of innovation, requires the ability to collaborate and share ideas with other people, and to sit down and talk with customers and get their feedback and understand their needs.'
>
> —Bill Gates

Those leading or facilitating innovation programs within their organisation need to be aware of not lumping all initiatives into the same program. At another organisation, we generated a considerable volume of suggestions; the team collated and facilitated the exploration of these within the organisation. Upon completion, ideas to be progressed were categorised as something to:

- **Implement now**: This makes sense and aligns to our organisation's agenda.

- **Concrete suggestion**: This is likely to be implemented within a year. The idea needs to be further refined and socialised, possibly matured. This also aligns to the organisational agenda. Further, you tend to be over optimistic of what can be delivered (many of these ideas ran beyond a year).

- **A dream**. This is exciting; however, it is unqualified and likely to take several years and iterations. The Tesla learnings need to be applied to the dream.

Whenever considering **dreaming** in an organisation, determine if:

- There is a product niche with a small market willing to pay a high price for the first iteration.

- There is a mid-market that will be excited by the next generation of product. Your product is probably not going to be the cheapest; however, it must be differentiated. Is this mid-market a niche?

- Is there a possibility of this differentiation becoming mainstream? The business could then scale. Be mindful that scaling attracts attention and niches don't.

Often there is a desire for scale but the niche may be more lucrative, if you could make it profitable and sustainable.

Warning on Design, Lean and Agile

These terms are used interchangeably by people at all levels within organisations as they seek to explore, trial or implement new ways to work.

Design Thinking

This is a great way to get closer to customers. What problems do the customers have? Design Thinking is an obsession with identifying, framing and establishing solutions to problems.

Lean Start Up

Lean Start Up is a way to develop businesses and products without being wasteful. Frequent iteration is central to the process with the intent of meeting initial customer needs, reducing risks and avoiding considerable costs of traditional launches.

Agile

This refers to taking the software development process and applying it to other types of work. Often, organisations confuse themselves with the term 'being agile' and the 'practice of Agile'. Additionally, organisations think that if they 'practise Agile', they are indirectly also integrating Design Thinking and Lean Start Up. This is rarely the case and with large traditional organisations, it's probably highly unlikely.

'Practising Agile' leverages the incremental development of software that emphasises:

- Individual and interactions over processes and tools.
- Working software over comprehensive documentation.
- Customer collaboration over contract negotiation.
- Responding to change over following a plan.

The above is known as the Agile Manifesto[12] set out in 2001, and it's great when applied appropriately.

Agile *WARNING*

'Practising Agile' is now being overplayed by organisations as the path to reducing the risk of disruption. If you implement the 'Agile' without understanding the pain points of customers and qualifying a business model, your organisation runs the risk of doing the same work in an 'Agile' manner.

Consider a traditional company that has implemented being 'Agile' at scale; however, it continues to be eroded by the services and products of emerging competitors. The traditional organisation is potentially cycling through the wrong work in a more effective manner. This is why Pre-Digital Assessment (PDA) and Responsibilities, Activities and Initiatives (RAI) need to be considered by organisations. If you choose not to do these, how can you check? Simply asking your 'Agile' team about their 'backlog'. Is this more of the same? If it is, the traditional company's situation could be exacerbated.

If it's not yet clear, 'Agile' is not *being agile*. What? By having the practice of 'Agile' within an organisation, teams are empowered to make decisions; however, this does not convert to *being agile*, that is, moving quickly and easily. There are benefits in being agile.

> 'An organisation's ability to learn and translate those learnings into action rapidly is the ultimate competitive advantage.'
> —Jack Welch

If you are worried about disruption, you need to first consider how you differentiate. Why not set a challenge to think more often and do less?

Partnerships

There is and will continue to be considerable investment by technology companies for digital business technologies. There is a difference between information technologies: the technology that enables organisations to send email and use applications to digital technologies. Digital business technologies will be smart and enable smart services.

Here is a glimpse of a possible future. It is 2020 something, and you are walking along the street. You have a slightly sore arm from playing that technology game with your grandchild. It is amazing that cricket can now be played in the living room—your glasses convert to a gaming screen, the walls become the crowd at Lord's. Your grandson won despite your ability to select Warne's ball of the century during a tense session (if only Mike Gatting had this game to train with prior to Warne's first test match in the UK).

The glasses you are wearing are advising that an appointment has opened at your physio. Your diary had checked your availabilities earlier that day and waited for any change at your preferred physio. You blink and accept the appointment with a confirmation appearing on your glasses. The glasses now calculate the time and distance to the physio, automatically re-shuffling your commitments for the day and advising others of a change in schedule.

In the distance you hear an ambulance, everyone around you looks at each other: why the nervousness? Somebody's smart connected clothing has indicated they are about to have a heart attack—that sore arm was a sign of something bigger and fortunately, you will be treated prior to any significant health impact.

The purpose of sharing this story is to show the integration of technologies and how they could potentially be integrated into the products or services your organisation offers. There will be an intersect between your analogue business and the emerging potential of digital. The ability for your organisation to create the digital product or service is limited; however, partnering with a technology company to deliver something is possible. The challenge is selecting the appropriate partner and this is when things become a little tricky.

'When I meet with founders of a new company, my advice is almost always: Do fewer things. It's true of partnerships, marketing opportunities, anything that's taking up your time. The vast majority of things are distractions, and very few really matter to your success.'

—Evan Williams

Large technology organisations provide many businesses with information technology services. Very often, the people representing these organisations are not the technical experts, they are sales and marketing people, and they have a target to achieve. Your organisation needs to select a range of possible partners based on your digital potential (more about this later) and present your intent of your relationship with these organisations. This process requires some competitive tension and should be aimed with the objective of obtaining sponsorship for your organisation and the specific initiative from an executive outside of sales and marketing.

Technology executives will sponsor initiatives when:

- An idea is good.
- There is a team of people who will partner as peers with their team.
- They have confidence in the capability of the individuals within the organisation.

Many organisations become frustrated with those organisations providing technology services due to the lack of ingenuity. Often the issues reside within the organisation searching for the service. So before embarking on deepening your relationship with a technology partner, consider asking:

- Are they working with others in this capacity?

- What attributes do these organisations have?

- Would they consider working with you and your organisation to explore possibilities?

This conversation should be undertaken with several organisations, making sure not all your eggs are in one basket. These arrangements are potentially for larger organisations. I have seen great sponsorship beyond the immediate team and how this greatly assists in establishing what is possible as several specialist resources meet.

A big learning for anyone transitioning into a leadership role is dependency on 'others' for outcomes. Micromanagement is not sustainable, good people will leave and you will become exhausted. The 'others' are beyond your immediate leadership team; they are potentially across the organisation and external to your organisation. Sometimes first-time leaders adopt a very combative approach with those external organisations that serve them. Initially this may have some cost benefit. However, over time value is almost always diluted.

One of my former employers was one of those external organisations. They have amazing people that served their clients in an exceptional manner. I was fortunate to be included in many client interactions as my colleagues built out relationships and solutions. The approach was not transactional. It was more like a dance—clumsy at first yet almost always ending elegantly.

The dance was a negotiation. As a technology leader this is 'some of your role'. For others that serve you, it's 'all their role'. As a technology leader you need a structured approach and a sequence of steps:

Who are the key players from the vendor?

- *What level of influence do they have within their organisation?*

- *How is the organisation and the individuals serving you performing for their performance year?*

- *How important is your business to them?*

- *If possible, at the initial meeting get to know them as people beyond their role at the organisation. Take an active interest in them and be professionally personable. This will serve you well later.*

After you know the key players, what are their motivations and goals from your emerging deal/partnership?

- *Beyond the dollar value, how important will your business be to their profile?*

- *Is there anything new/innovative within the deal? How proven is this? Could this be an area of mutual value?*

- *What has been/will be automated or simplified? What are the benefits for the vendor and your organisation?*

The focus is not about winning, it is about growing the value of the deal and creating as much value as possible.

- *This is value for both organisations—not dollar value (neither size nor margin). It is what is in addition to this.*

- *Involve others in these conversations, apply lateral thinking. Often within technology deals a partner is involved, ask what could be of value for them.*

Take a break. Based on what you now know, when would you *not* proceed?

- *Document what you know, your baseline. Be prepared to walk away if the deal is below the baseline.*

What is the window to reach possible agreement? The bigger the reasonable window the better the negotiation. If you are wanting to pay 10 and they are requiring 50, it's unlikely; however, 40 to 50 is possible. What is your baseline? If this is unlikely to be met, it's potentially best to walk away. At this stage consider:

- *What is high value to the other parties but low value to me? Consider making concessions on these.*

- *Endeavour to grow the value for the technology provider and its partner.*

How can value be grown further? Explore this with all parties.

Reflect on the progress. Is the deal good for all involved and can it avoid win/loss agreements as long-term value is eroded?

- *Only proceed with a win/loss agreement if it is a one-time negotiation. This is the only time you should consider winning. However, you need to consider the reputational risk of this action also.*

- *Potentially check separately with the technology partner. Sometimes partners come under pressure from technology providers so make sure there is value for them within the deal and that they can fulfil their commitments.*

Finally, consider the number and timing of the concessions you could make. This is important as not everyone will be as mature in their approach:

- *Three to five concessions are ideal.*

- *Don't lead with the best concession or your baseline, as people need to feel like they are going to win or have won. Sometimes they will need to report back that they have won.*

- *Put in padding to make sure you know where you could make concessions but be sensible and not ridiculous.*

- *Technology providers and their partners are expecting some negotiation. On some occasions, conversations or relationships becomes tense so consider taking the heat out of them by having a personable conversation.*

In summary, as a first-time technology leader, seek to build genuine long-term relationships with an objective of creating value within your organisation and across those that serve yours. The approach to these negotiations helps; however, you will also need an understanding of the type of person you will be interacting with, as this can help you avoid cycles. As a former Technology Executive across multiple industries, I have met many people who were keen to interact and transact. Some of these people were truly awesome and we remain in contact today. Frustratingly, on the odd occasion, I found other types of people:

- Mother-in-law: A necessary relationship but with limited possibilities of improving it.

- Upstart: Optional relationship, talks a big game; however, not sure they can deliver it.

- Player: Flirts with the potential of an enduring partnership; however, once the sale is made interest is lost, then the 'B' team arrives.

- Outlier: This person is more aligned to your organisation than theirs, what we discussed is never possible.

- Timewaster: This person is more interested in meeting their KPI for client contact. They are unprepared and as a result you are unlikely to meet with them again.

- Pedestrian: More of the same and the individual or organisation are potentially now on borrowed time. If the potential of their services is beyond the existing arrangements and I have an opportunity I will ask their organisation to change this person.

- Kool Kat: They arrive at your organisation in black t-shirts or something similar; they look out of place and appear to have disembarked the train at the wrong station. We are not cool; it appears we could be wasting their time and they explain how cool they are. Their suggestions are not practical and are disconnected from reality. They leave and return to their club at cool cave.

- Professor: Clever but disconnected. This person is interesting to listen to; however, there is no relevance for your organisation.

- An in-law's in-law: This is a forced relationship, probably not of your choosing and something that must be complied with. Make this as painless as possible.

Confidant is the ideal type. These people listen and understand. They offer experience to help; they are prepared to invest time; they work to your timeline and not their quarterly targets.

The list has more controversial than constructive types. Everyone wants a *confidant* but that doesn't mean you will be with this person all the time. They will orchestrate activities across their organisation. They are humble, accepting and constructively collaborating with your other partners. Sometimes they uplift other partners, this is outstanding and always remembered.

Confidants are more likely to be key contributors to digital possibilities.

Innovation recap

Every organisation is striving for some form of innovation. This will vary in extremity. Regardless of this:

- Set the **right conditions to encourage** diversity of thought, flexibility, casual connections, idea evolution by experts connecting, simplicity and structured creative collaboration.

- Consider how your **vendor community** can help with **delivery of tactical innovation** that is likely to involve task simplification, processes, data insights and integrated teams with different reporting lines.

- There will be several vendors who will be **selected partners for strategic initiatives**, dream together and **identify technical capabilities of one another.**

- Agile is not *being agile.*

PART 5

DIGITAL

Simplifying the digital complexity

All organisations need to consider three areas for their digital potential:

- Timing: A product or service rather than the whole company should be identified.

- Clarity: How will this enhance the customer relationship or enable scale in a digital ecosystem?

- Duration: What will be sustainable?

There are many studies, books and papers on this topic, many of which have been reviewed by me over the last five years. There are three publications/studies that have remained with me and form the final stage of the D-I-R-T-Y model; coincidentally, two of these originated at MIT.

> 'Lots of companies don't succeed over time. What do they fundamentally do wrong? They usually miss the future.'
>
> —Larry Page

These two studies are important for organisations realising their digital potential and for understanding how and why it is important:

- Organisations that have achieved successful digital business models have outperformed industry average profitability by 25%.

- There is a significant need to identify, establish and sustain differentiation in a dynamic digital landscape.

- As mentioned earlier, transformations generally fail. Transitions are better and these studies when integrated offer clarity on where to transition.

Prior to diving into action, it's important to understand some broader aspects. The reality of situations is based on perception: there are ecosystems that need to be understood. Maybe your organisation doesn't need to be the disruptor and there are various uses for Technology, Customer, Operational and Information and they need to be managed differently.

Contemplating digital

There is tendency for organisations to determine and prioritise actions based on a bias of experience and input from trusted colleagues. Often, senior colleagues have a subconscious bias to trusted colleagues, favouring those who validate their thinking. The emergence of digital will require different and new thinking within any industry; it presents both an opportunity and a risk for all organisations.

The Santiago Theory of Cognition[13] is helpful in creating a greater consciousness of the system people participate in—not a technology system or process but the broader ecosystem. When reading this think about the ecosystem.

- Cognition emerges as a consequence of interactions between the system and its environment. Cognitive systems can be technology or 'living' systems.
- Technology does not rationalise reality, there is no bias.
- The essence of Santiago's theory is that we do not perceive the world we see; we see the world we know how to perceive.
- In a situation where there is conflict (conflict can be good), there are different systems with different realities.

If somebody endeavours to explain a situation based on their reality, they may refer to this as what is 'really going on here'. The person explaining this is making a demand for obedience: 'what I see is real and you're delusional'.

- If this is not understood, the state of the system is delicate for those involved.

If a group accepts and initiates those items relevant for them in the D-I-R-T-Y model, it will be operating with little hierarchy and much humility. This sets an example for colleagues that nobody can see everything that is occurring, and everyone is learning. This is a reminder of the growth mindset principle but specific to digital as people may endeavour to interpret what is occurring.

'The one thing that sets us apart is the fact that we are always self-critical. Because having success today doesn't mean having success tomorrow. It's like your footprints in the sand at the beach. When a wave comes, it gently erases all your steps from the past.'

—Zhang Ruimin

Learning and openness are two key enablers as your organisation contemplates and initiates digital initiatives. Remember that any person's reality is not actual reality. For example, *my reality is not reality, it is a perception, and we need to learn together.*

If you apply Santiago's theory to how people within organisations are contemplating digital, you will discover that if they are not a learning organisation the consequences could be significant. If digital is a significant business objective, organisations need to consider who makes up their leadership teams.

Often the Chief Information Officer (CIO) reports into an executive role rather than being a member of the executive team. Therefore, if a digital conversation occurs within an organisation at the board or executive level, it occurs without a technology industry professional.

Based on my experience, there are three types of CIO:

- **Technical:** This CIO is comfortable and confident with their technical nous and can be found coding or provisioning infrastructure. Their background is within technical roles and limited business experiences. There is a belief that any technical scenario can present an opportunity to create a better solution. The risk for the technical CIO is they work 'in' technology rather than 'on' the business.

- **Procurer:** This CIO has arrangements in place or are making the arrangements for the delivery of services from a third party. This can present opportunities such as automation of infrastructure to the cloud but also risks such as outsourcing of traditional services and projects to third parties. When establishing or being within an outsourcing relationship, there is a risk that the third party will be measured/rewarded on the delivery of services rather than evolving the service. The implications for the broader business receiving the services is stagnation or expensive iterations (yes, iteration, not innovation) via change requests to evolve the service. Degradation of technical currency is the outcome.

- **Business:** This CIO considers the technology team an extension of the business rather than a service provider. They understand, clearly contribute to and co-create parts of the broader business strategy. They link the possibilities of a well performing information technology capability with emerging or established operational and customer technology.

These technology leaders operate and contribute to the system but they need to understand their bias. If you are a CIO and you identify with one of the above types, consider how 'learning your biases' could contribute to how you evolve in your role and offer a greater contribution.

Peter Senge, who authored *The Fifth Discipline* originally published in 1990, explores the learning organisation and systems thinking. Systems thinking links interdependence and interconnectedness. A good example is family. A family is a system. Often a situation within a family is a symptom of a broader problem; therefore, a poorly behaving child is a symptom of a broader problem. Potentially, the child is seeking attention or replicating behaviour of another family member. Senge's work explains that there are many points of interdependence and interconnectedness at many levels across society. These points of 'inter' are now global and commenced being global in the Industrial Age. The digital possibilities for an organisation to integrate systems, not just technology; digital is part of our society's evolution. Digital is part of the evolution of your organisation, business unit and people.

The CIO role is only part of the system and should be a contributor to digital rather than owning digital. The management of digital will be different from organisation to organisation based on how a CIO manages information technology due to the many 'inters'.

Senge's book includes a section on 'loops', reinforcing and double loops that are useful for systems thinking. When sharing this concept with clients, start with analysing a loop from their perspective. (However, the broader perspective will offer the greatest contribution, hence the earlier section on Santiago theory.)

- A reinforcing loop is an action by one party, creating a responding action by another party, and then continues with actions by both. An example is the arms race between the USA and USSR, with both countries stockpiling weapons as a position of power. A reinforcing loop is a system cycle that continues, the cycle could be good or bad.

- A double loop is a loop where one action creates an alternative loop. In my workshops, I use the example of a community with a crime problem. Crime occurs within this community due to an illegal drug dependency. The police endeavour to address the drug problem by arresting known drug dealers, intervening in the reinforcing loop between crimes occurring and drugs being purchased. This seems like a sensible intervention; however, due to the number of drug dealers being reduced, drugs are now less readily available, the price of the drugs increases followed by an increase in the volume of crime. It's important to note that not all actions can be positive.

Systems thinking and the learning organisation need to be understood by an organisation. Loops and actions need to be studied by organisations. The potential of digital can enhance or exacerbate a situation rapidly and as we are still in the early stages of digital the exacerbation is unknown; however, I believe it will be significant. This is different to the threat of disruption. The potential consequences of disruption are an elimination. Systems thinking can create variances over time. These variances need to be understood by an organisation. Systems can be iterated.

Transitions are better than Transformations

Many organisations struggle when considering going digital. To determine what is digital for them? What digital means for their existing business? Often, they wait to see what others are doing for digital, adopting a fast follower mindset.

Language and modern terms confuse many non-technical and, in some cases, technical executives with what their organisation could be doing and how they should be doing it. There is no clear path to digital, rather a range of shifts within three states.

Years of research on transformations has shown that the success rate for these efforts is consistently low: less than 30 percent succeed. *This year's results suggest that digital transformations are even more difficult. Only 16 percent of respondents say their organisations' digital transformations have successfully improved performance and also equipped them to sustain changes in the long term. An additional 7 percent say that performance improved but that those improvements were not sustained.*[14]

Prior to these states, consider the following:

- Most transformation projects fail.

- Organisations are reluctant to enter considerable transformations. This, I think, is completely reasonable.

- Transformation outcomes are not clear. Often, the perceived outcomes of the transformation are unknown until it is progressed after considerable investment.

- Transformations often measure milestones prior to a go-live rather than outcomes.

Organisations considering digital need to determine if the effort will require a transformation. Potentially, the longer an organisation waits prior to commencing a digital initiative, the greater the possibility of a transformation project. Consider what you should start now for the future. The probability of the transformation project being successful is unlikely based on history.

> 'I don't want to fight old battles.
> I want to fight new ones.'
> —Satya Nadella

It's sensible to do something now. How?

There are three modes that should be implemented consciously by an organisation:

- Existing/Traditional Business: This is to be maintained and not neglected. Refining and not stagnating this business is important. The first four stages of the D-I-R-T-Y model (working backwards) are important. Lurching into D and eroding the existing business is not realistic for most organisations. If the organisation believes there is no other choice, the probability is that they waited rather than acting on something in an earlier period.

- Interim Business: This is an explorative mode to seek outcomes that may enable a digital future. The intent of an interim business mode is to qualify possibilities by outcomes rather than milestones. Establishing a transaction capability that is automated is a milestone, the use of this capability is an outcome. The frequency of use increases the outcome of being an appropriate mode for digital.

- Digital Business: This is implementing an interim business. In the majority of instances, the existing/ traditional business will continue to evolve and be complemented by the digital business.

There are techniques to enable organisations to consider how they could implement the above modes when they have an existing business.

Initiating transitions

Regardless of the type of business, a great digital business consists of customer intimacy and global scale. They are potentially dichotomies; however, within an exceptional digital organisation, they are not. A frequent and potentially over emphasised example is Uber. Organisations strive to be like Uber, so let's use it as an example to apply the above two factors.

- Uber has closeness to its customer through location and previous trip data. They also know what type of customer you are by the rating the driver applies.

- Uber has a digital ecosystem with a supply chain: a driver, car, location and passenger. Much of this is automated and integrated; it is an ecosystem.

Uber continues to be studied by mainstream, traditional organisations. I am often asked by organisations to help them be more like Uber because they want to be the disruptor. This is possible; however, the likelihood of us both forming a meaningful longer-term business relationship is unlikely. In reality, this is not possible as your organisation would probably need to be in another time and industry to achieve this.

Further, you need to consider who are fatigued with the talk of disruptors. The disruption effort, in many instances, has happened, probably with success around the edges of your business. However, this doesn't stop statements being made by leaders or those with influence, and these are often whispered, mumbled and repeated by others: 'we need to be more like a disruptor'. Are you sure about this? What is feasible and reasonably sensible? Here is a hint, maybe you don't need to be the disruptor; let's assume this is the case.

What if all your competitors were focused on being the disruptor and not the disrupted? What is their or your likelihood of success? How many start-ups fail? Lots! Often, venture capital will not be made available to those who have not failed or failed multiple times. Large organisations don't like failing. As mentioned earlier, many organisational transformations fail (like 80–90% depending upon the study). If start-ups and transformations fail, what could be an alternative?

What if your organisation was one of only a few thinking alternatively?

What if an organisation thought about segmenting its focus and effort with technology?

Here is a suggestion: make it a stretch but not ridiculous. Start with a walk and build to longer, more frequent sprints. Be practical and apply some sensible principles. Many organisations tend to treat all their technology efforts the same. There is a big focus on Agile. As mentioned earlier, an expansion of Agile within organisations is sometimes the easy substitute for creating innovation. Agile will help with doing the work; however, it's unlikely to change the type of work. This may be a working methodology; however, there will need to be some decisions of the objectives.

While we are talking about delivery modes, Gartner has lots of clever people who think and write about many things. Gartner introduced the 'Bimodal' approach to technology, accelerating selected explorative initiatives and managing other predictable initiatives. I have worked with many teams who applied Bimodal and it was effective.[15] However, with the breadth of technology emerging across organisations, there is a greater level of thought prior to action required and this needs to be structured.

There are three possible purposes of technology within an organisation.

Information Technology

This is the traditional IT department consisting of infrastructure, network, applications, data and security. This can be contained and managed within many enterprises. Their operations evolved with the emerging software as a service (SAAS) cloud technology, sometimes employees opted in for SAAS without informing IT; however, the application was soon isolated or integrated. Further, there is the emergence of devices, which began with employees bringing a device to the device being provisioned within an organisation or managed by a software solution. Both instances are known as shadow. IT teams are not great at managing technology that is initiated externally to them. These IT teams have been successful in helping employees shadow technology sometimes after being dragged to the table to do this.

Operational Technology

This helps a business perform by automating manual activities. For example, cleaning a floor in a shopping centre or a driverless train in Paris's metro. Operational technology is common in manufacturing. The scale of operational technology may enable customer technology. For example, smart transport: informing a commuter of the best possible commute home or where to not walk in a shopping centre.

Customer Technology

This is generally enabled by a mobile device and application. However, it is expected to evolve to an experience. The probability of near field communication recognising your device and prompting something that you are interested in is now occurring.

Each of the above scenarios present different challenges and opportunities for organisations within different industries. Consider the following:

- An information business, like a professional services organisation, is more likely to have more information and customer technology whilst considering its automation options with operational technology.

- A manufacturer, who will have information, operational and possibly some customer technology.

- A service provider, who will have customer, possibly operational technology although likely to be partnering with another providing operational technology.

Using our earlier example, Uber is often referred to as one of the most successful digital businesses due to its customer intimacy and global scale. The emphasis of the ecosystem potential resides with operational technology and the intimacy with a customer will be achieved with customer technology (obviously). When organisations are considering priorities, there needs to be an awareness of digital era success factors and purposes of technologies.

The innovation within an organisation may be to initially identify and focus on the emerging options of each technology purpose. Rather than wanting to be the next big disruptor, seek to shift the organisation with a structured assessment of Customer Technology, Operational Technology and Information Technology.

Finally, the approach to security will be similar for each technology purposed; however, the consequences will be different:

- Customer Technology: The theft of information being made publicly available is likely to erode the reputation of an organisation.

- Operational Technology: Being penetrated is likely to disrupt the internal performance of the organisation (production of product) or the orchestration of services offered.

- Information Technology: IT is likely to result in the theft of information, which will compromise organisational knowledge and potentially disable the organisation for a period.

Good security practices will also need to evolve as the organisation evolves. Organisations are excited by the prospect of technology but need to incorporate the appropriate security. Ensuring the appropriate security investments are forecasted and implemented as timed will enable the broader progression of technology. Choosing not to do this will inevitably lead to a security risk manifesting in an issue. This may still occur when the investments are made; however, the remediation of the issue is likely to require considerably less effort and cost.

> 'In a digital world, the gift I give you almost always benefits me more than it costs.'
> —Seth Godin

Further, the risk of stagnation due to the security scheduled activity and investment not being completed will present business issues. These business issues will result from being unable to proceed with the broader technology agenda as the security team is playing catch up. If this situation remains for a period, the issue—over time—could extend beyond the management of the technology to larger market and commercial issues.

Digital business

There are three factors that will determine when and where to act: Market, Digital and Differentiation. I developed the MaDD model by integrating some great thinking from others.

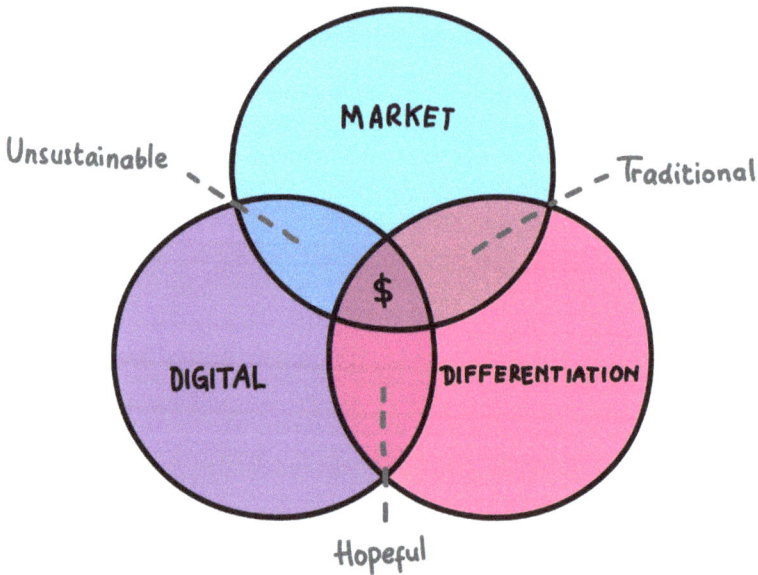

Figure 8: MaDD model

When all three components are met, you will have a viable digital business. This business will probably commence in parallel with your traditional business. Over time, the digital business may or may not become the primary business; digital may be part of the business. Regardless, it's unlikely your existing business will remain in its current form.

The 'Market', S-Curves and timing of actions

In Geneva in 2002, I met Dr Theodore Modis, the author of *Natural Laws in the Service of the Decision Maker*. I was sent on a mission by my employer to review his S-Curve software and consider how this could support some decisions the management team was considering. This trip and his work have remained with me. It is applicable now, as it was then, for organisations to endeavour to anticipate, prepare and execute activities for products and services.

> 'The great thing about fact-based decisions
> is that they overrule the hierarchy.'
> — Jeff Bezos

Dr Modis' work is intended to assist businesses by linking known management practices to the S-Curve principles. S-Curves complement rather than replace management practices. The S-Curve is a simple model and qualifiable with data. It removes human bias. There is a cycle: a beginning, a growth phase, a maturity phase, a declining phase and an end. Metaphorically, it is like the seasons beginning and ending with a second winter.

When S-Curves are combined with Systems Thinking, there is an opportunity to improve decision making. There is an acceptance of the stage of a business and the natural laws of a cycle. S-Curves assist in the anticipation, preparation and decision making within an organisation. Acknowledging the stage of a business assists in determining the course of action that has the probability of a good outcome. Invest in those in spring and replace those in autumn.

There isn't one rule for any organisation. There will be various decisions within an organisation based on the stage of businesses within it. There are simple laws that have broad applications that enable efficiencies. A business that is in growth phase may be complemented by a digital initiative; a business that is in a declining phase may best be treated by being replaced with a digital model.

S-Curve seasons and digital decisions

Season	Digital	Approach
Spring	Complement	The business is in growth phase and a digital offering should complement rather than replace the existing business.
Summer	Optimise	The business is mature. Efforts should be focused on optimising the existing business and making the most of the summer season. Can a digital offering extend the season?
Autumn	Incubate	What can be salvaged and experimented within the existing business? What could be digitally trialled to potentially jump winter and enter a new season?
Winter	Innovate	What are the alternatives to the existing business? Have any digital players entered your market? How could you innovate beyond their offerings?

Table 1: S-Curve seasons and digital decisions

The above considers the stage of a business. Some of these businesses may not be digital; therefore, wanting to disrupt your business may be bad business.

'Digital' business models focus on scale and customer intimacy through technology.

The first MIT study to consider is *What's Your Digital Business Model?* It was undertaken by Peter Weill and Stephanie L. Woerner who are both MIT digital research leaders. The opening sentence of the book states that 'digital transformation is not about technology—it's about change. And it's not a matter of if, but a question of when and how'.

This study is comprehensive and includes 50+ workshops for C-level executive teams and a survey of 334 enterprises. In the workshops, they noticed that the greater the digital disruption, the more radical change needed to be, since the enterprises and teams struggled to make decisions for themselves.

The risk is that an organisation will lurch into a digital initiative, seeking to be the next disruptor. Based on the history that most transformations fail, the S-Curve could be applied across the various businesses within an organisation resulting in informed decisions being made. The study validates that the objective of a digital business is to have:

- Greater customer intimacy, referred to as getting closer to end customers.
- The digital ecosystem moving, referred to as moving from supplier models to digital ecosystems.

Many of my clients are existing businesses and are considering how they integrate or introduce digital into their business. There is an uncertainty of what digital could be for their business and industry. These organisations often have multiple businesses within them and each of these are at different stages. When deciding on initiatives for their organisation, there is a tendency to experiment with digital initiatives rather than determine the preferred type of digital initiative. Decisions like this are based on a feeling and not on fact.

The MIT study also identified three key capabilities to compete in the digital economy. What can your organisation do to compete in the digital economy with one or more of these capabilities?

- Content, products and information.

- Multi-channel and multi-product customer experience.

- Internal and external digitised platform.

How? Enterprises can master these capabilities by:

- Refreshing and enriching content that will drive new sources of revenue.

- Ensuring superior customer experiences that will create cross-seeking opportunities, resulting in increased revenue per customer.

- Developing digitised platforms that will enable economies of scale for better margins.

S-Curve seasons and digital initiatives

Season	Digital	How
Spring	Complement	Content products and information. Refreshing and enriching content to drive new sources of revenue.
Summer	Optimise	Multi-channel and multi-product customer experience. Ensuring superior customer experiences that will create cross-seeking opportunities, resulting in increased revenue per customer.
Autumn	Incubate	Discuss if the business should continue as it is, don't fight the seasons and look for greater ROI of digital initiatives in other businesses. If digital is an option, consider developing digitised platforms that will enable economies of scale for better margins.
Winter	Innovate	If viable, move to a digital business incorporating scale and customer intimacy. If digital players have entered your market, resulting in an early winter, how could you innovate beyond their offerings? If this is not possible, exiting the business may be the best decision.

Table 2: S-Curve seasons and digital initiatives

If you have a business in the second half of the season cycle, you need to determine if you invest in or learn from it. This is important as not all businesses will be affected equally by digital.

Weill and Woerner's research found that large enterprises with more than $7 billion in revenues have the most to lose; wherein, executives estimate that an average of 46% of their revenues are under threat. Why is this the case? It's due to their hefty profits and inability to change rapidly.

If you are a small business, it's good news. Weil and Woerner explain that small businesses are effective at digital disruption because of their ability to create strong connections with their end customers and their ability to partner with other companies and suppliers.

Finally, and not surprisingly, customer mobile engagement is particularly important. Those organisations that focused on this and achieved their goals had net margins and revenue growth of between 5.5 and 6.1%. Mobile forms part of the customer strategy; the purpose of mobile initiatives will be subject to what season the business is in.

'Differentiation'

This is a topic discussed within many organisations and is a key learning from attending IMD and MIT's Driving Strategic Innovation. This was my highlight of a week of learning and was the second piece of MIT research completed by Duncan Simester (2017). Traditional market frameworks are outdated; a digital lens is now required for differentiation.

The framework includes six areas of differentiation. When you reflect upon these, it is quite evident how organisations can become overconfident and then confused. Here are my key notes on differentiation from a very detailed presentation and subsequent conversation:

Costs

- You may not need to be the lowest cost as long as you can differentiate—your mobile phone is a great example. Cost is important in markets where there is no other source of differentiation.

Brand

- Brands are different subjects to their market. Customers will look at the product or service and go beyond the brand. Generally, the product or service is more important than the brand. Think about your mortgage and what is more important: the financer or a low rate with some possible features?

Relationships

- What are your organisation's relationships and how exclusive are the arrangements? Who controls the relationship and what are the consequences for your organisation if the relationship fails?

Human capital

- The most overrated point of differentiation is it can be easily replicated. If this is your differentiation, it's not sustainable.

Switching costs

Switching costs is possibly one of the most undervalued. A control study was carried out on two retailers who contacted their competitors' most loyal customers. Competitors targeting a retailer's customers made those customers more loyal to that retailer by driving up sales of their product.

Here is what to assess:

- How easy is it to do business? Ease of ordering and transacting can make customers 'stickier'.
- The on/off switch: When a customer decides to switch, it is a big effort that effectively locks them into their new provider.
- You want a 'sticky' group of customers for yourself but also for your competitors as this can help alleviate price competition.

Your greatest risk, in this scenario, is a new entrant at a lower price.

Market share

Market share may represent both past and future differentiation. Can the past make it easier to satisfy future customers? If there is a 'switching cost', then past market share may provide a strategic resource in the future.

Further consider:

- The extent of a positive external network used by others. For you to interact effectively, you have little choice but to align.
- The past strength of a brand can drive future success; however, this probably needs to be supported by expert endorsement.

Certain differentiators will benefit certain seasons. If costs are the only differentiation early in the season cycle, the business will be difficult to sustain. Cost differentiation introduced in the winter season could potentially extend the duration of the cycle.

S-Curves and differentiation

Season	Digital	What to differentiate
Spring	Complement	Relationships: who controls the relationship and how exclusive is this?
		Brand: how does your product or service differentiate?
		Switching costs: ease of transacting and the ability to then lock them in?
Summer	Optimise	Relationships: who controls the relationship and how exclusive is this?
		Switching costs: if a customer decides to switch, is it a big effort?
Autumn	Incubate	Switching costs: you want a 'sticky' group of customers for yourself but also for your competitors as this can help alleviate price competition.
		Market share: do customers have little choice and are they required to align?
Winter	Innovate	Costs: can you sustain differentiation beyond being the lowest cost?
		Market share: can your past strength drive future success with a digital business model?

Table 3: S-Curves and differentiation

Some of these may seem obvious; however, they should not be ignored. It is important to assess each component of differentiation, timing and possible digital initiative prior to deciding on a course of action.

A nimble organisation will increase the probability of being successful in the digital realm. Digital is not a single destination;

rather, it relates to many iterated destinations, and the choice of destination(s) is determined by what future will be most relevant for your business.

> 'If I had some idea of the finish line, don't you think I would have crossed it years ago?'
>
> —Bill Gates

Digital recap

The final recap begins with another important reminder of mindset:

- Santiago Theory: *your* **reality is not** *my* **reality** and we all need to **learn** together.

- Systems Thinking includes reinforcing loops and double loops; **not all actions are positive**, and these are **likely to be exacerbated** in a digital world.

- **Transitions are better** than transformations, as most transformations fail.

- Digital outcomes should **achieve greater customer connection** and create an **integrated ecosystem**.

- There are **three types of technology: Customer, Operational and Information**. Their importance will vary subject to the type of business.

- Use the **MaDD model** to establish where, when and how to **introduce digital**.

CONCLUSION

This book is about change. That change involves people, technology and digital business. I share my professional experiences and thoughts and reference the work of others. Their integration created the D-I-R-T-Y model. The model is not a prescriptive schedule for implementation; however, each section should be a prompt for exploration and conversation.

Connecting with a broader range of people matters; they are the spark for your digital future. The potential of this will be achieved through the quality of your people's and external partners' contributions. This will not be a single activity, it will be a series of them beginning with the rationalisation of work, transparency of the technology, uplifting of risk capability and integrating of innovation that will ultimately lead you to consider your digitisation. Digital decisions will incorporate the factors of timing, clarity and sustainability.

There will be small steps in each section. These steps will contribute to transitions that avert the need for transformations and create sustainable change within organisations. In addition to the digital transition, it is highly likely that a transition capability will be created within the organisation.

IN CLOSING

If you want to learn more, visit:
www.changelead.com or
www.davidbanger.com.

If you would like explore how you
could initiate a program, make
contact at david@changelead.com
or +61 (0) 406223352.

Initially, David will spend 90
minutes with you (at no cost) to
explore your organisation and its
potential. Example areas that may
be discussed are as follows:

- An organisation recognises that opportunities are being
  presented in its market(s) with potential consequences
  for not acting.

- COOs whose value chain is changing and where
  validation is required for existing, emerging and possibly
  more radical options.

- Greater customer intimacy through the enhancement of
  products and services with relevant technologies.

- A CIO, CTO or CDO seeking to drive a digital business
  program that enables future business models.

- Review and optimisation of legacy practices to realise the benefits of automation and rationalisation of technologies.

- Selection or commencement of sensible digital innovation initiatives while qualifying longer-term aspirations.

- Aligning dispersed teams for the program delivery of several large or multiple interdependent projects.

- Value realisation of partner and vendor ecosystems within existing or new arrangements by accessing their global scale.

David is an advisor to executives, mentor to technologists and a digitiser for your business. He is an excellent facilitator of large strategic workshops linking strategy to technology, innovation to outcomes and business objectives to digital. He has spoken at many industry events and within organisations. The models within this book change conversations and initiate transitions.

REFERENCES

Dweck, C. (2007). *Mindset: The new psychology of success.* New York: Ballentine Books.

Isaacson, W. (2015). *The innovators: How a group of hackers, geniuses and geeks created the digital revolution.* New York: Simon & Schuster.

Modis, T. (2013). *Natural law in the service of the decision maker.* Switzerland: Growth Dynamics.

Morgan, J. (2017). *The employee experience advantage: How to win the war for talent by giving employees the workspaces they want, the tools they need, and a culture they can celebrate.* New Jersey: Wiley.

Senge, P. (2006). *The fifth discipline: The art and practice of the learning organisation.* London: Random House Business.

Simester, D. (2017). *Capturing value: What have we learned from observing firms' attempts to differentiate.* Cambridge, MA: MIT Sloan School of Management.

Skillicorn, N. (2019). *What is innovation? 15 innovation experts give us their definition.* Retrieved from Idea to Value: www.ideatovalue.com/inno/nickskillicorn/2016/03/innovation-15-experts-share-innovation-definition/

Watzlawick, P., Weakland, J. H., & Fisch, R. (1974). *Change: Principles of problem formation and problem resolution.* New York: Norton.

Weill, P., & Woerner, S. (2018). *What's your digital business model? Six questions to help you build the next-generation enterprise.* Boston: Harvard Business Review Press.

ENDNOTES

1. https://en.wikipedia.org/wiki/Six_Sigma
2. https://en.wikipedia.org/wiki/DMAIC
3. https://en.wikipedia.org/wiki/Ada_Lovelace
4. https://ethw.org/Integrated_Circuits_and_the_Space_Program_and_Missile_Defense
5. https://hiring.workopolis.com/article/how-hewlett-packard-defined-the-startup-work-culture/
6. reference https://en.wikipedia.org/wiki/Robert_Noyce
7. https://www.internetlivestats.com/total-number-of-websites/
8. https://en.wikipedia.org/wiki/Jorn_Barger
9. https://en.wikipedia.org/wiki/Blog
10. https://en.wikipedia.org/wiki/History_of_the_Encyclopædia_Britannica
11. https://www.tesla.com/blog/mission-tesla
12. https://en.wikipedia.org/wiki/Agile_software_development#The_Agile_Manifesto
13. https://en.wikipedia.org/wiki/Santiago%27s_theory_of_cognition
14. https://www.mckinsey.com/business-functions/organization/our-insights/unlocking-success-in-digital-transformations
15. https://www.gartner.com/it-glossary/bimodal

ACKNOWLEDGEMENTS

Firstly, and most significantly, I would like to thank my wife, Nicole, for her love, support, and wisdom as we share our lives together. I would also like to thank my children for their interest and excitement in my 'book project', and my parents for their quiet guidance, particularly my dad, who always demonstrates the right thing to do.

During my life, there have been families with whom I have been fortunate to share experiences. These families were actively involved in those 'special occasions' and helped with those testing times. They all shaped who I am today. These families, and their decade of significance, are the Blenheim family being my mother's family (1970s), the Wybenga family (1980s), who were our neighbours and are like family, the Kindos family who welcomed and loved me (1990s), the broader Calder family who are my European-based family and godparents to our children (2000s), and those within the Murrumbeena community who have become like family to us (2010s).

Lastly, a special mention to my publisher, Sylvie Blair, and editor, Jo Yardley, for making the book possible.

www.ingramcontent.com/pod-product-compliance
Lightning Source LLC
Chambersburg PA
CBHW041734200326
41518CB00020B/2591